What I Learned from Balanchine

George Balanchine in rehearsal with Melissa Hayden and Nicholas Magallanes, ca. 1957–58. (See copyright page for full credit line.)

What I Learned from Balanchine:
Diary of a Choreographer

by

Gloria Contreras

Translated by K. Mitchell Snow,
Lucinda Gutiérrez,
Roberto Mata

Edited by
Daniel Shapiro

Jorge Pinto Books Inc.
New York

What I Learned from Balanchine:
Diary of a Choreographer

Published by Jorge Pinto Books Inc. Website: www.pintobooks.com

Translated from the Spanish by
   K. Mitchell Snow, Roberto Mata, and Lucinda Gutiérrez
Edited by Daniel Shapiro
Cover design by Susan Hildebrand
Book design by Charles King. Website: www.ckmm.com

Cover Image:
Gloria Contreras. *Huapango*, New York, 1959. Photograph by Rafael.

Frontispiece:
George Balanchine in rehearsal with Melissa Hayden and Nicholas Magallanes, ca. 1957-58. Photograph © Martha Swope. Choreography by George Balanchine © The George Balanchine Trust. BALANCHINE is a trademark of The George Balanchine Trust. Courtesy of New York City Ballet Archives, Ballet Society Collection.

Inside Photos:
Photograph (p. 103): by José Luis Arreguín
Photographs (pp. 109, 111, 112, 113, 120): © Martha Swope
Photograph (p. 119): © Lourdes Almeida
Photograph (p. 121): by José Murguía
Photograph (p. 122): by Gabriel Eduardo

ISBN: 1-934978-02-7
978-1-934978-02-3

Contents

Introduction

Gloria Contreras, the founder and director of the Taller Coreográfico de la UNAM (Universidad Autónoma de México), Mexico's most important neoclassical dance company, spent her formative years as a dancer and choreographer in New York City. There, she studied with George Balanchine at the School of American Ballet.

Contreras had left her native Mexico in 1955 to join the Royal Winnipeg Ballet on the recommendation of Madame Leminsky, an examiner at the Royal Academy of Dance who had seen her perform with Joaquín Pardavé in *Orpheus in Hell*, choreographed by Guillermo Keys for the Fábregas Theater. A year later she moved to New York, where she began taking ballet lessons, but she was soon forced to return to Mexico for health reasons. She concluded that dancing in a conventional ballet company was not for her.

At the encouragement of her father, she returned to New York in 1957, almost penniless, and lived with a Puerto Rican family in Harlem. She then moved to the Brandon Club in Manhattan and supported herself with the help of The Salvation Army. She became a frequent visitor at International House, a foundation that presented regular activities for the city's culturally diverse student population, where she met young people from all over the world.

During this time, she was attending classes at the School of American Ballet, where she met and was profoundly influenced by George Balanchine. She created her first five pieces—*El mercado* (The Market), *Huapango*, *The Wise and Foolish Virgins*, *Vitálitas*, and *Ocho por radio* (Eight for Radio)—which formed the core of her New York company, México Lindo. This company, which soon became known as The Gloria Contreras Dance Company, performed her pieces from 1958 to 1970. Contreras returned to Mexico in 1970 to found the Taller Coreográfico at the National Autonomous University in Mexico City.

What I Learned from Balanchine has been adapted from letters Contreras wrote to her parents, in diary form, from August 1958 to October 1959—a crucial stage in her life, both personally and professionally. The diary records the artist's struggle to belong to the world of neoclassical ballet during her early adult years. It also traces her series of encounters with George Balanchine that were to prove so fruitful to her.

—Lorena Luke Contreras
Lorena Luke Contreras is the author's daughter.

The Beginning

In mid-1957, I arrived in New York to continue my education in dance. I went to the School of American Ballet, where I began to take classes. I often visited International House, where festivals were organized for the residents—students from all over the world who attended Columbia University and who represented their countries through dance, music, and theater.

I was soon invited to participate in the events at International House. I formed a small group of students from the School of American Ballet with whom I put together a program that I called "México Lindo." I choreographed my first piece, *El mercado*, with music by Blas Galindo, for that program. That was how my work as a choreographer began. I later followed up *El mercado* with *Huapango*, using music by José Pablo Moncayo. The subsequent performance at International House was so successful that my group won an award from Columbia University.

From my experience with these two works, I realized that choreography was my calling. Some time before this I had obtained George Balanchine's phone number from Dr. Henry Jordan—who was Tanaquil LeClerq's doctor as well as my own—and I now called to ask him for an appointment. He agreed to see me and my group on August 1, 1958. We were given "Room B" at the School, which was located on Broadway and 83rd Street. Mr. Balanchine arrived punctually and watched us perform my works. Afterwards, he said to me: "If I have to sign a document that certifies that you're a choreographer, I'll do it. But you don't want to be a choreographer, you want to be a poet."

From that day onward, the School became my home and my laboratory. The administrators lent me rooms whenever they were available so I could rehearse with my dancers. They gave me a pianist—Gordon Boelzner—and allowed me to work with the students at the School. That was the beginning of a small workshop that lasted six years, during which I choreographed many pieces, including some that Mr. Balanchine commissioned for the New York City Ballet.

Now, after more than 38 years of continuous work with my company, I have created more than 200 original compositions that have been performed internationally. I give my ongoing thanks to

Mr. Balanchine, the School of American Ballet, and the magnificent dancers I've worked with (some of whom appear in the photos accompanying this diary): Their generosity has helped guide me in my chosen path from those early years in New York to the present day.

—Gloria Contreras

The Diary:

August 1, 1958–October 26, 1959

1958

August 1

Today was a very important day in my life. At two in the afternoon, George Balanchine entered the studio of the School of American Ballet with the sole purpose of watching my choreography. I hadn't expected him to be so punctual. I was sitting on the floor soaked with sweat from my last rehearsal but his simple manner inspired my self-confidence. I greeted him amiably and introduced him to Alek Zybine; he already knew Loi Leabo and Marlene Mesavage. We danced *Huapango* for him. He said that in his opinion, the music is a Mexican version of what is being done in Hollywood. He added that the popular themes are very beautiful but that the symphonic arrangement kills them. He also criticized the orchestra, which he thought was bad and insipid, at least in the recording.

His words were more or less these: "The beginning is good and promising, the development is original and has an air of mystery but suddenly you jump to an *adagio* that isn't very original. It doesn't suggest anything new. In the 'little sparrow hawk' variation, there are good moments, but you get caught up in the melody and don't create imaginative figures. The choreography for *Huapango* demonstrates your love of dance, but this isn't everything. You must produce for the audience, not only for yourself. Take an idea, analyze it, and make thousands of variations on each theme. Create an image and turn it inside out. Give your dance a motif. For example: a man who can't separate himself from his other self, his ego. He appears from the wings wrapped in this other body and no matter how hard he wrestles, he can't disentangle himself from it. With this idea, you can suggest a lot to your audience. One man might imagine that he's her spouse, whom she hates and whom she can't separate from. Another, that it's the terrible part of himself that he can't cut off, even though he wants to. Someone else may think that this is what he needs, someone always at his side who won't let him feel lonely. Something else you might develop is a *pas de deux* in which neither he nor she can take each other by the hand. Create a handicap for yourself and in the struggle to resolve it you'll find figures never used before. What is a *glissade arabesque*? Anyone can use it and create choreography from it. But you don't want to do that. You're the new generation, I'm the old, and you should find your generation through choreography. You could sell this work (*Huapango*), but what good would it do you? I'll tell you: none. You already master basic composition, you know how to put a group of dancers together, you have a good ear, and you're very musical. But you also have the mind and the talent that demand the kind of work that stands above the crowd. Don't try to compose over the melody, harmony, rhythm; that's the atmosphere you want to work with, the richness with which you should develop your inventions."

Then we danced *El mercado* and in his opinion it was much better, because it had more steps that I'd invented myself and wasn't derived from pure technique. He suggested that I do more with the *rebozos*: Form a single body with the three dancers whose arms are different colors, move them in different directions and with a different sentiment, turn their backs to the audience, and in one moment show only their three faces, etc.

After the rehearsal or audition, whatever you want to call it, Balanchine waited for me to pick up my things and we went to a small studio. He shut the door and we talked for an hour. We even danced together, trying to solve problems like that of the *pas de deux* in which the dancers' hands remain behind their backs. He asked me why I wanted to choreograph and was pleased when I answered that it's fascinating to work with bodies and mold them according to their personalities. He told me that in his company there were several people who'd approached him and said "I want to be a choreographer because I know that I can't do any more as a dancer, and besides, being a choreographer is a good job."

Balanchine hates this way of thinking and he doesn't want me to produce because I "ought to." We agreed that a complicated storyline kills a ballet and that the only form in choreography is the body, which it molds. "In my house," he said, "I'm the carpenter, I play the piano, and I like to cook." He hates to choreograph for dancers who only care about virtuosity and applause. We spoke about *Agon*, his emotional state while he was creating the ballet, and my impression upon seeing it. I showed him our album and talked to him about our shows. He saw the photo of Jorge Cano and liked it very much. I put in a good word for him so if he auditions some day, he won't be unknown. We spoke about Marlene Mesavage and he said that he'd take her into the company when he thought she was ready to join. He wants me to work with the music of Revueltas. In his opinion, he's the most talented Mexican musician. He likes

Chávez and is interested in his *Toccata for Percussion*. He remembered the Campobello sisters and is surprised by my work because I come from a country that has very little stimulus for dance. He gave me permission to attend all of his rehearsals, as well as those of Jerome Robbins. He wants me to study music, sculpture and painting and never to commercialize my work. "Show me everything you produce and promise me not to sell anything that isn't going to last on its own artistic merit."

Balanchine's words possess so much knowledge that it's necessary to record them on paper. His confidence in me is worth more than anything. Balanchine is a rare individual. He's a sophisticated person who doesn't like simple things or melodies for the masses. He wants me to produce something different. But he also thinks that I have more value than a simple Broadway choreographer or someone from "X" company. He doesn't want me to run, but to study and continue producing. There is much genius in him, but even more humanity.

It was a good day, which was a recompense for our six daily hours of dance and our tired muscles, in short, our small sacrifice. I only want to add that Balanchine told me "If I have to sign a certificate that says you're a choreographer, I'll do it. Your work is grammatically correct, but you want something more than grammar. You want to create poetry. It isn't the meaning of each isolated word that produces poetry but the manner in which the words are put together. Well then, create poetry, poetry in dance."

August 6

I've thought a lot about what Balanchine said and I think he's right on many points. My work isn't elaborate enough for his complex sensibility. My choreography is my self-expression and as a consequence, is simple, childlike and happy. My first rule is to be sincere, to tell the truth, and this is my truth: to be simple, like a melody, without the complexity of counterpoint. I'm going to follow nearly all of his counsel, but I'm not going to try to be "original." I believe that the instant I give up being myself, trying to reason with the likes of Jerome Robbins or George Balanchine, I'll lose whatever value I have. His basic problem with *Huapango* was its lack of strange steps and the use of what he considers "his generation." "Create dance in a new form, one never used before, that has joy in every instant, in every figure." This is all well and good, but for the time being I have to study and live fully. My work will evolve as I mature.

This week I've been a little tired and lazy. I'm not happy with myself because I haven't done anything yet. I ask myself, how much music do you know, how well do you understand the painting, music, and sculpture of your time, what do you know of Picasso or Stravinsky? Nothing. My knowledge about culture is so scant that a breath would carry it away. I want to do so much and I don't really do anything. My dancing isn't very good, either. The summer course didn't add anything to my technique. I'm very ambitious and I get desperate. Next week I'll begin to study ceramics. I have no idea how capable I'll be of creating something with my hands, but I'll give it a try. Monday I'm going to have dinner with Lincoln Kirstein, the director of the New York City Ballet.

August 7
I didn't go to class today. One of my feet is waging a small war against me so I went to see Dr. Henry Jordan. What I have is nothing serious. Dr. Jordan is a great person. I took him the leather portfolio I got him in Mexico and he liked it very much. He sees me and he treats me like a daughter.

Tomorrow I'll speak with the Mexican consul; it looks like we will dance for the Mexican community on September sixteenth. I wrote Felipe Segura without receiving a response. I hope I can find out what he thought. I get desperate when I think that all that work might have been in vain. He wants to premiere *Huapango* and *El mercado* on September sixteenth and he wants me as the guest artist. But I didn't even get a brief note in response to my letters. If I don't go to Mexico or to Brussels, I'll work here for the Mexican community.

I went to a record library and listened to the *Toccata for Percussion* by Carlos Chávez. It made a great impression on me. During the entire work I felt a great emptiness in the pit of my stomach. Afterwards I listened to the *Sinfonía índia*, also by Chávez, but I didn't like it as much as the *Toccata*. To understand Balanchine, I listened to the music for *Agon* by Igor Stravinsky but it was simply intolerable. I know that the reason for my reaction is my immaturity and ignorance, but it still seems like a miracle that Balanchine was able to create such extraordinary choreography from this work. What I'm writing now will surely seem sacrilegious in a few years, because I've proposed to improve myself through study, which I've already begun. Today Balanchine wants me to produce "cubism," but before I can arrive at that point I need to pass through all of

the preceding stages. I think my current work is simply expression-
ist and is a long way from being abstract. I've read a lot of Juan
Cristóbal, about the lives of Beethoven and van Gogh. Van Gogh
is the closest thing to God.

August 12

I've thought all week about Balanchine's words and I've come to
the conclusion that I must be "Gloria" first; originality will come
with my intellectual development and life experience. I must live
and study intensely and continue my choreographic experiments
until I can give the public ballets that express art and humanity. As
for my girls, they don't speak with Balanchine; when they have to
they become pale and sick to their stomachs. I'm the only one who
has a "man to man" relationship with him. The others act like slaves
before their lord or men before God.

Last night I was invited to a dinner with Lincoln Kirstein, the
director of the New York City Ballet. He's written many books about
ballet and is founder of countless institutions, among them the ballet school I attend. He's a cultivated, wealthy Jewish man, friendly
and spontaneous in his actions. He speaks with absolute authority.
He arrived on the roof terrace of International House, where we
were waiting to have cocktails with him. Among the others in the
group were a South African singer with a degree in criminology;
a Japanese student of plastic arts; a literary Indian woman; the
American painter Tom Kendall; Bob Verbenkmoes, a producer and
artistic director; and an American dancer.

The first few minutes were uncomfortable until Lincoln and I
broke the ice. For more than three-quarters of an hour, I carried
on wonderfully and brought up topics of great interest to him. We
spoke about Mexico, Chávez, the current art scene, etc. I also told
him about myself and my group. Then we began to disagree. He
thinks it's impossible to use folklore in dance and believes that an
artist can't interpret a specific folk dance from another culture—for
example, Marlene dancing a *jarabe*. As far as painters are concerned,
he prefers Siqueiros and I like Orozco, but we were completely
at odds about Moiseyev. When he heard that the company's performance had pleased me, he leapt up and called it "a cabaret act
without any artistic value." Despite the fact that everyone was on
his side, I maintained my position and rebutted his argument.

But then my loquaciousness stopped and I kept quiet for the
rest of the evening. Tom Kendall, who likes my work very much,

was nervous because I didn't tell Kirstein about my interview with Balanchine. He spoke up for me and when Kirstein was saying good-night, he told me that he expected to see me at the rehearsals. It was an agreeable moment: succulent food and a good connection. I have no idea what kind of an impression I made, but maybe it wasn't a bad one. Men like Kirstein must become bored with the people who agree with their opinions all the time and they probably respect someone who speaks his or her own mind.

August 13

Yesterday I had an appointment with Consul Aguilar to discuss the celebration on September sixteenth. A representative of the Mexican Center who has to decide whether or not to use my group was there. Don Manuel is a great "Godfather" and always does what he can to help me. His first question was "Has your economic situation improved?" Later he said that he'd write to Miguel Alvarez Acosta. I told him I'd need a minimum of $400 for a two-hour program; a staff of at least 10, at $30 each; and $100 for set costs, etc. Then, this "friend" began to beat around the bush and said that he doubted that the project would be approved because the maximum budget allotted by the Center for the celebration was $60. Consul Aguilar said that if I were the one presenting the show, he could invite the consuls of other countries, but that if it were someone else, he wouldn't tell anyone. In the end, the "friend" agreed to speak with the Mexican Center and resolve everything with me tomorrow. In the meantime, I'm beginning to make the preparations. The place I found for rehearsals is in the consulate and is very satisfactory; I'm also looking for people. I've asked my parents to ask Humberto what costumes are necessary for the *jarabes*.

Later that afternoon we went with Don Manuel to Roberto Mendiolea's apartment. According to the consul, this man could become the next director of Bellas Artes. He's a great friend of López Mateos, the president of Mexico. He writes and composes, is intelligent and works well with people. He's now at the United Nations, conducting research for López Mateos. He's in contact with Mexican musicians and through him I'm going to get the latest recordings of Revueltas, Galindo, etc. Tatanacho will bring them to me when he returns from Mexico on the 20th. We were in his house until nine at night and we agreed to get together to make music when Tatanacho arrives. Mendiolea will present the speech ("El Grito")* on September sixteenth. In prior years, Andrés Iduarte would have been the speaker, but this year he's going to be in Mexico on that date. Next Tuesday Lou† and I are invited to eat at Manuel Aguilar's place. Yesterday I had a tough rehearsal and I'm doing whatever is necessary to find male dancers.

August 16

The New York City Ballet Company returned on the twelfth after an absence of six months, during which it performed in Japan, Australia, and the Philippines. Yesterday we celebrated with Judy Friedman. I decided to organize my tribe to welcome and cheer her up. Because she gained weight on the tour, she won't be dancing with the company during its New York season. Our group of ten drove 50 miles to a beautiful place in the mountains full of weeping willows, all kinds of flowers, houses of modernist design, and a lake. We arrived about eleven at night. Despite the rain, we cooked in the garden. We had the classic American food—hamburgers. There was also vodka, gin, and lots of sweets. I'd brought all my records, record player, maracas, etc. Judy had told us to bring pajamas and swimming suits so we could stay overnight and enjoy ourselves all day on Saturday, boating and skiing, etc. I was very excited, and despite my exhaustion I was able to liven up the party. We missed Pascual Navarro, but in his place we had Kenneth Dewey, who sang and played the guitar. I danced and we clowned around with jazz rhythms. Ken sang *La Bamba* with an accent and got very red when I flirted with him. He got so distracted that he kept losing the beat.

Judy told us about Japan, Australia, and Manila. I feel badly about Judy. I'm going to try to create a new ballet with a big part for her so she won't feel so sad. She asked me to take her into the group again, and, of course she's welcome. She's a good dancer but she's too heavy for Balanchine's company. I don't blame Balanchine. I think his purpose is to create a first-rate company even if that makes a few people suffer. When you try to give the audience the best, you have to put sentimentality aside and if Roberta is the best-looking and has the strongest technique, then Roberta deserves the job. Balanchine seems indifferent to my dancing since he learned that

---

* The official "cry" of independence, commemorating the 1810 "Grito de Dolores," delivered every year in Mexico.
† Louis Luke, the author's husband.

9

I'd gotten married. I work hard without the hope of achieving much. I often wonder if I'd take myself on as a contractor.

Thinking about my time in Mexico leaves a bad taste in my mouth. But Mexico is child's play compared with New York. Here the atmosphere is as bad as there, but New Yorkers have achieved a certain "refinement" in causing suffering. Nevertheless, not everyone suffers. Judy has had bad luck, but it's the opposite for Joysanne Sidimus, my other dancer. She has a good place in the company and is happy. The same thing happened with Janet Greshler, Victoria Simon, and Sara Leland. All five entered the company at the same time and only Judy has to leave. Maybe the company will take on Marlene Mesavage as an apprentice. I hope so. She needs the work. Reading Dostoyevsky has been a tranquilizer for me but it's only now as I write this that I've been able to get out of my bad mood. I've been having insomnia lately. As for my foot, the bone is OK, so I won't need to go under the knife.

August 21

The Mexicans have decided not to use my group on September sixteenth, despite the minimal cost of our program. It consists of a two-hour performance, with ten professional artists rehearsing three hours a day for a month; this includes the cost of sets, lights, costumes and music. We're asking for $400, which is what each one of the dancers would earn if my group belonged to a union. Consul Aguilar is very upset with the Mexican Center. So is Espíndola, and he's taken this so much to heart that he asked me to help him with his "vendetta," which would consist of mounting my program in Carnegie Hall. To do this, I'd need at least two additional works and the appropriate costumes for each dance: ten from every region. Despite the "No" from the Mexicans, I've continued rehearsing my group. I need to get it back into shape so we can audition again. We rehearse from seven to ten at night in the Mexican Consulate because Don Manuel is my Godfather. The women dancers are Vera, Eleanor, Loi Leabo, Marlene Mesavage and Judy Friedman. The men are José Aruego, Carlos, Kenneth Dewey, and probably Gino.

In the mornings I've been taking class with Robert Joffrey. He's the best teacher in New York, but also the most expensive. Each class costs me $2.50, plus $1 for transportation and lemonade, which totals $3.50. That hurts.

August 23

Bob Joffrey is a wonderful teacher. If I took classes with him regularly, I know I'd make progress, but he charges more than any other teacher in New York. Today, after his class, we had a rehearsal. We finished mounting the *Jarabe largo*. This is a new group and it took them three nights to learn it. It still needs a lot of polishing, of course. Next week the rehearsals of the New York City Ballet begin and I hope the directors let me watch. Balanchine took on two new dancers, one from the Ballet Theatre and the other from Robert Joffrey's company.

August 26

I've gone to the New York City Ballet's rehearsals all this week. I'm the only person outside the company who's allowed to enter. Three days ago Balanchine began the choreography for a *pas de deux* to Tchaikovsky's *Violin Scherzo*. He finished it today. In all, he worked for eight hours and fifty minutes and it's beautiful: completely romantic, lyrical and technical. It runs for about ten minutes during which the dancers move constantly. It's only the physical endurance and perfect technique of Patricia Wilde and André Egelvsky that make the *pas de deux* danceable. At the beginning, all the steps look easy but are actually excruciating to execute. Today the violinist, the orchestra director (Robert Irving, ex-director of the Sadler's Wells Theatre), Balanchine, and the dancers all worked together.

Watching these artists combine their talents provides a great example. They all work with equal intensity. I'm learning not only about choreography but how to be a good dancer. Patricia Wilde is always ready, attentive, amiable, and respectful even if she's falling off her feet. She never marks. Every time she dances she does so with technical purity and elegance. Egelvsky, even though old, is still "Egelvsky," but despite his countless pirouettes and great technical skill, my eyes always go to Pat; that's because this ballet, and even more, romantic ballet, is a feminine art.

I also saw *Apollo*. Balanchine created this ballet when he was 27 years old. The choreography is embroidered around the music of Stravinsky and it's completely modern. It fascinates and obsesses me. Yesterday Allegra Kent learned the *adagio*, and even though I've never danced it and perhaps never will, I learned it just by watching. It's extremely interesting to note that some of the figures are similar to those of *Huapango*. Because of that, I now understand clearly why Balanchine thought I was using what he called "his generation."

I don't mean to say that my ballet is comparable to his, on the contrary. It is only now that I've had the opportunity to analyze his work in depth that I can see why my ballet didn't satisfy him. But it's a coincidence that without previously having seen *Apollo*, I've broken similar technical rules.

Yesterday I gave Balanchine a kiss. At the end of the rehearsal for *Apollo*, I was in a feverish state. My hands were sweating and I was agitated. Without even thinking, I went up and kissed him. Balanchine told me that when it premiered, the ballet was criticized as absurd. It's only now that people are beginning to understand it. Today I will see *Apollo* and *Agon*. I'm anxious for the hour of the performance to arrive.

September 1

Last Friday I sent a note to my parents asking for my violin. I'd just returned from the rehearsal for *Agon*, which completely amazed me. At the end, I approached Balanchine and told him, "I can't even speak after what I've seen, and I feel that I'll never be able to choreograph anything worthwhile after this." Beautiful and affectionate as he is, he took my face in his hands and caressed me, telling me not to worry. He went on to comfort me by saying that he'd started when he was fifteen years old and that now he was fifty-four. Through study and work I would fulfill my dreams, he assured me, but first I had to learn music. When I mentioned that I'd studied a little violin, he told me that, in his opinion, knowing the violin was even better than knowing the piano, and that I should also take classes in harmony and writing. I replied that I'd thought about it but that I didn't have enough money and that I never wanted to stop attending all the classes at the School of American Ballet. "Of course not," Balanchine said, "you must be a better and stronger dancer than all the people you work with. You should never depend on their technical capacity, but with your talent and superiority you can strengthen them. Regarding the tuition, I'll speak with the school and we'll see what we can do because I'd prefer to see the money you're spending here invested in musical knowledge. You shouldn't choreograph in order to sell or become famous, but in order to acquire knowledge for the future."

Tomorrow, the City Center season opens and I'll be able to attend all of the performances. Balanchine spoke with the woman in charge so they'll let me in. My dreams of the theater and of entering the company must be postponed to accommodate my studies. "You need at least three years of intensive work in music," Balanchine said. I think he's right. Before I can call myself a choreographer, I must study hard.

September 7

Thursday I went for a massage but it was counterproductive because when all my nerves and muscles relaxed, I felt the weight of two years of work. I went straight to bed and despite being totally worn out, I wasn't able to sleep. I was in real pain until I finally dropped off. An hour was enough. I awoke feeling in perfect health and went to the New York City Ballet. I entered through the back door, where Barbara Horgan gave me a company dancer's pass. I went with Judy Friedman, who was very sad that she was there only as a spectator. I really hope the company takes her back.

The performance wasn't the best. The company is in bad condition because many of the best dancers are out for different reasons. Nevertheless, we saw a first-class *Apollo*; then *The Firebird*, by Stravinsky, danced by Melissa Hayden. She is wonderful, but the ballet is a traditional tale that doesn't suit my tastes. *Pied Piper* and *Fanfare* are two light ballets by Jerome Robbins. They're very good and were well danced.

I've been working on *El mercado* and *Huapango*. Every day I see more clearly what Balanchine was trying to tell me. I know that I must rework some parts. The sequence with the *rebozos* is now complete. I've developed it using the "canon and fugue" form, in other words, a theme performed by the dancers, beginning with each one in a different beat and with small variations on the theme. Another part that I've revised is that of Laura Urdapilleta, the harp, in *Huapango*. The essence is the same but it's much more elaborate. The down-side is that we get tired-out working during the day and at night we can't rehearse as we should.

September 10

I don't have enough time to do anything and when I realize what day it is, it's already mid-week. I've worked a lot but still haven't begun to study. Last night I went to see the premiere of the *Pas de Deux,* which Balanchine choreographed for André Egelvsky and Patricia Wilde. I was as nervous and emotional as if Balanchine had done a piece and all because I was present during the work's creation. It's lovely but nothing more, and to be honest, I think it will be danced for a few years and then sent to the archives. Patricia Wilde danced marvelously.

I'm working on *Huapango* and have modified it so much I think it's become a different ballet altogether. I don't know whether I'm improving it or making it worse. Yesterday I went back for a massage and this time I didn't feel sick, only tired. But it was good for me and today my muscles feel better. I still haven't secured a scholarship at the School of American Ballet because Balanchine is busy with the season and hasn't stopped by the school. Nevertheless, the secretary told me that I shouldn't worry about my pay until Balanchine speaks with Mrs. Ouroussow. Regarding the violin, I think that my father is right and I should get myself an old piano.

September 11
I used the time between my two classes today to do some chore-ography. I'm very tired but something happened today that helped me gather new strength. In the first class, a guy named Fredo came up to me and told me that I was dancing very well. He went on to say that I "would definitely become a ballerina." Of course I'd be delighted to be elevated to the rank of *ballerina*. Knowing that someone values me raises my spirits.

September 14
I've been working on the choreography for *Huapango*. Mendiolea requested the score to *Toccata for Percussion*, by Mexican composer Carlos Chávez. We'll begin to study it. I enrolled in the YWHA, the Young Women's Hebrew Association. Judy Friedman took me there and they accepted me immediately even though I'm not Jewish. It's supposed to be a good place to study music. I enrolled only in music theory because Judy wants to be my piano teacher. I'm not too excited about the idea, since classes taught by friends are never formal, but she was so insistent that I found it impossible to say no. The academic year will cost me $45—one class per week for 35 weeks.

September 18
On Sunday night, Judy Friedman was taken back into the company. On Saturday we'd taken class together and she told me she was going to Montauk for the weekend. I don't know why she changed her mind and decided to stay in New York. When they called her at seven-thirty and told her they needed her to dance that very evening, she simply flew to the theater and got everything she asked for. It's her second performance in New York; she danced in four of the

pieces that evening, two of which she'd never performed before. She learned them during the day and danced them very well. Strangely enough, however, when I went to the dressing room, I found her crying, disappointed in herself. She was certain that her performance had been a disaster. Dancers! We're never satisfied. It reminded me of the evening following the Fábregas show: My father had to listen to my soliloquy in the car, my laments and cries of dissatisfaction. As usual, I'm of two minds about this. On the one hand, I'm happy that they took Judy back into the company. On the other, I'm sad because I'm losing her again and she won't be in my company.

Today we received the good news that Marlene Mesavage will be taken on as a permanent member of the company in a couple of weeks. Until now she's been an apprentice, but she's been called up because of the chaos that the New York City Ballet is going through. All of the ballerinas are sick or indisposed: Melissa Hayden sprained her ankle, Diana Adams pulled a tendon, Tallchief is expecting, Joysanne re-sprained her Achilles' tendon, Sara Lelan a muscle, and the list goes on.

Allegra Kent has been elevated to prima ballerina and received the most eloquent review that the most severe critic, John Martin, has ever written. I felt vindicated since I'd foreseen this a year-and-a-half ago; it surprised me that they, the critics, didn't notice her talent, which was so obvious to me.

Esther Villavicencio is leaving for Chicago tomorrow and has a contract to dance in the opera directed by Ruth Page. Yesterday I went to register for my piano classes. Now all I need is the instrument. I won't study in the Young Women's Christian Association, but in the Jewish one. They're more musical. Despite the fact that everyone in the world is receiving contracts except for me, it's a fact that I'm making progress. What serves as an excuse for any other person to give up only stimulates me more; I'm realizing just how much I have to overcome to be able to triumph. I have faith in myself because I have faith in God.

September 20
I've become addicted to reading again. I finished *The Diary of Anne Frank* and now I'm reading some wonderful legends about Mexican dance in *El folklore musical de las ciudades*. The legends are about Quetzalcóatl, Sacnité Anáhuac, and Moctezuma; and the feasts of Tlaloc, Xóchitl, Payambé, etc. They're very interesting and appropriate as sources for ballet. Of course, I'd have to contact a

good musician. I've been visiting Rodolfo Mendiolea, the former director of the Composers Society of Mexico and of the publication *Claridades*. He's a good friend and it looks like he'll help me get some music by Carlos Jiménez Mabarak based on Oaxacan folklore.

September 26

Last night, as I was leaving the theater, I ran into Janet Reed, who has been chosen as the new ballet mistress for the New York City Ballet. I asked her to keep me in mind in case there's an opening for an apprentice. It's embarrassing to have to be so forthcoming in the middle of the street, when you only have a couple of seconds, but there's no way of developing the conversation to the point of making such a request. If I don't act like this, I'll never act at all; opportunities to speak to Janet, or to Mr. Balanchine, are very hard to find, so you can't be shy about them.

In today's class, I worked so hard that I was completely drenched when I finished. I know I'm making progress. I note it in my posture, my extension and the relationships I have with the other dancers. Allegra, "The Kent," takes classes every day. I'm working on becoming as good as she is. Of course, that's a tall order but it's helping me improve my style and technique. Allegra has something that I admire very much: She personifies purity in dance. No mannerisms, no exaggerations, simply the purest line that dance is capable of achieving.

I've seen *Agon* several times. Unfortunately, it no longer produces the emotional shock it did on first sight. Now I see it from a distance and with the emotional equilibrium that allows me to analyze it objectively. In *Agon*, Balanchine has found a new form of plastic expression. He creates a thousand sculptural groups, all beautiful and modern. The commercial porcelain figurine looks corny when compared to one of these groups.

Today the people in the front office called about my scholarship. Balanchine had spoken with them and by common agreement they decided to grant it to me. It includes dance and Labanotation. They're also going to let me use one of the school's pianos until I get one. Tuesday is my first piano class, and Thursday I have Theory. On Saturdays I take Labanotation. I've decided to get up an hour earlier every day so I can get to school and practice for an hour before class.

September 27

The weather is glorious. I'm on the porch and I can see the blue, calm sea, that green garden splashed with boats that seem to be patches of different colors. The sun warms my cheeks: It makes me feel happy. The background music is the *Concerto for Percussion and Chamber Orchestra* by Milhaud. It's wild and exciting. I'd love to use it for a piece. I'm going through a critical phase, though I feel incapable of creating another ballet. I'm not sure if it's because Balanchine is so great that he makes me feel tiny, or if it's just fear. I hope that my talent is real.

I'm happy that Anita Cardús is dancing so well. Lupe Serrano is at the Metropolitan Opera House with the Ballet Theatre and she's dancing wonderfully. Nevertheless, John Martin hasn't written favorable reviews of her work. Next week I'll see her dance.

September 28

Every class I attend at the School of American Ballet is one point gained in my struggle. They're so important to me that my day isn't complete if I miss one. I've also been taking jazz and this week I'm starting with music, piano, and Labanotation. Marlene Mesavage is so happy to have become a member that she looks even more beautiful than ever. When she comes on stage, her hands freeze with emotion. She speaks with her eyes and smiles continuously; it's enchanting to watch her. Marlene looks great on stage, but Judy Friedman has more personality, despite her size.

October 1

Last night I went to a music store and bought a copy of Chávez's *Fifth Symphony*. The opening is perfect for a ballet. The entire work is beautiful, except for one small part, but it's extremely long, and it doesn't express happiness but sheer tragedy. I wanted to create a piece that suggests a small village fair, with dancers, vendors, crowds of visitors, a dance of the elders, masked participants, fireworks, a small bull, etc. But I can't find the right music. I purchased two other works: *Sensemayá* and *Cuahnáhuac*, both by Revueltas. I also bought Aaron Copland's *Salón México*, which I find unconvincing. Here in New York, you can find the works of Chávez and Revueltas, but nothing more. Both of them are great composers but their music is a bit too complex for me right now.

I've been sleeping poorly because I spend my nights thinking about ballet themes well into the wee hours of the morning, and then I create dance movements in my sleep. This morning I got up early and listened to several albums of Mexican music. At ten in the morning, I was practicing the piano in the ballet school, which has practically become my home. Pierre Vladimiroff's class was difficult and exhausting. Fortunately, I'm no longer ill.

After class, I shut myself up in one of the rooms to listen to music and think. At two-thirty I took my point class. I didn't know if I'd be able to dance, because of the callus on my foot, but when Janet Reed, the ballet mistress, came in to watch the class, I knew I had to dance and do it well. Fortunately, my foot hardly hurt at all, but I was so nervous that I couldn't do two or three pirouettes on point. My nervousness was so obvious that Janet began dying of laughter, until I actually fell. But all of a sudden, the door opened and Balanchine appeared. I immediately got control of my nerves and danced as well as I could; I did everything as if they weren't there and I didn't try any difficult steps. Then for the next hour and a half we paraded, one by one, before Balanchine, Janet, Vladimiroff, and Doubrovska, doing the most difficult steps ever invented for point. I smiled and danced and displayed my technical abilities as well as my personality. The competition was tough. But even so, my successful display didn't change the fact that the other fifteen dancers had also demonstrated their talent. At the end of the class I was dead-tired and soaking wet, but I was happy because even though I'd started out poorly, I was able to pull myself together.

October 2

My life was made for struggle, work, and daily improvement. This is what gives me energy. In Mexico, the slow rhythm and an atmosphere ruled by jealousy and hatred conflicted with my basic temperament. The people I was working with began to consider me an impossible case. I thought that the reason everyone disliked me had to do with *me*. I was surprised to learn that I'm actually good with people. My smile opens doors and my manner allows me to become part of all the families I've met. Here in New York, I've found the right atmosphere to develop, the right teachers, inspirational models, and close relationships with great people and great artists.

October 3

I'm listening to Flamenco songs and soaking my feet in hot water and Epsom salts as I write. I have a soft callous between my toes that's so painful it's making me see stars. I went to see a pedicurist and found out that the callous was infected, but not seriously.

Last night I went to the Metropolitan Theater and saw two famous Latin ballerinas, Alicia Alonso and Lupe Serrano, in *Giselle*. Alonso had the lead role, accompanied by Youskevitch. The first act was good, but not as wonderful as the audience seemed to think. Alonso had recently been in Russia where her *Giselle* was highly acclaimed. The response of the New York audience—clapping furiously after each and every movement Alicia made—was a little off-putting. She did well in general, especially in the mad scene, but I found her facial expressions a bit exaggerated. The second act was tremendous: Alicia danced perfectly, with fluidity and grace. She demonstrated that she's one of the great dancers of our time. Lupe Serrano played "Mirtha," the queen of the Willis. This role is rarely danced well. It's an extremely difficult part that requires constant leaping. Lupe danced it brilliantly. Few ballerinas have her lift and extension. Her acting was also good. The audience liked her, but they loved Alonso. Youskevitch gave a solid performance. Despite his age, he still exhibits a clean technique no longer common among dancers. I took exception, however, to his triple *cabriole*—in my opinion, he should have opted for a double. His virile and gallant acting made for a magnificent "Albrecht."

The first number was *Variations for Four* with choreography by Anton Dolin—a ballet that strives to be in the *pas de quatre* tradition. The choreography is unimaginative—it's nothing more than a simplistic display of technical steps and a contest of virtuosity, and the music is in the worst taste. For an amusing contrast, you can see John Kriza in one role and Erik Bruhn in the other. The latter is one of the best, if not the best, dancers of our age. Kriza plays a cowboy dressed up like a prince who's incapable of extending a knee or closing a fifth position. The other parts are played by Scott Douglas and Royes Fernández, both very good dancers, especially the latter. The last number was Jerome Robbins's *Interplay*, which I didn't like. I've just seen the New York City Ballet's version and the comparison is painful. It should have been saturated with jazz but I didn't see a hint of it in the dancers' movements. Ruth Ann Koesum was cold and reserved, and Enrique Martínez was awful. Technical problems can't be resolved with smiles, and Enrique simply doesn't move his body harmoniously. This is my review of what I'd call "a night of theatrical ballet" by the American Ballet Theatre.

October 4

In the morning, I went to see Doctor Berkowitz, who gave me medication for my foot without charging me. At nine-thirty, I started my dance-notation (Labanotation) class. The teacher is Anne Hutchinson, considered one of the authorities on the subject. The class is made up of 15 children aged eight to ten . . . and me. I'm taking the children's class because my schedule doesn't allow me to take the adult course. I felt a little ridiculous allowing myself to be treated like a baby. I ran through the room in a rapid rhythm and then moved my body slowly, in time to an *adagio* alongside my young companions. This in itself wouldn't be strange if the setting didn't feel so much like a kindergarten class. Nevertheless, I liked the class and learned something in it. It's a difficult subject and I think, to a certain degree, it will be advantageous for me to study it with children because the explanations are so clear that they stay with me and even if the pace is slow, it will be a good way to learn the subject. At eleven, I took class with Madame Doubrovska and gave my best effort. Sometimes I feel like I become tense in class because of my insistence on technique. At two I sat down at the piano and studied for an hour and a half.

Last night I saw Serrano in *The Black Swan*. Erik Bruhn was wonderful but Lupe's performance wasn't satisfying, despite the enthusiasm of the audience. She danced this same *pas de deux* in 1950 and it was perfect then. Lupe is still a great virtuoso, but she's adopted mannerisms, her attitude with the audience is proud and cold, and her technique is brilliant but not completely pure. I know that Madame Dambré would have given her a "puff"! The rest of the program was entertaining enough.

I found out that José, the dancer I've been training over the past few months and whom I was counting on for the Halloween performance at International House, signed up with the Ximenes-Vargas Spanish Company and is now in Florida. . . . Well, that's one less male dancer. Sadly, he was the only one.

October 10

Today I began my new ballet. I couldn't find any cheerful music, so I'm using the music to *Huapango* for the choreography. It tells the story of six girls who arrive very early at the site of a great village fair. At back-center is a church. Along the sides, in the foreground—it's kind of a ramp—are the stands. At one are displayed giant jars, each a different color, filled with fresh lemonade and other fruit-drinks. On the other side, candies, flowers, colored candles, garlands of flowers, and paper adorn the stands. The girls arrive dressed in colorful outfits with white, embroidered blouses. The new bride arrives, greets her friends, and introduces her husband, the groom. Suddenly, five or six elderly men enter, first to amuse, but then to frighten the girls with grotesque masks and canes. One of the girls attracts the groom's attention. A group of gossiping girls follows them and then returns to tell the bride. The bride is left dancing, alone and sad. A drunk upsets the *fiesta*, moving toward the bride and trying to kiss her. The groom, completely forgetting the other girl, approaches the drunk, hits him and embraces his wife. Both of them realize that they love each other, everyone begins to dance happily, and the fair goes on. "The End." The ballet requires enough dancers to play six girls, the two lovers, five old men, and the drunk.

After this piece, Judy Friedman, Raúl Roa, and Karen Morell will perform the *Jarabe pateño*, which I think I'll make a comic piece. Then the *Jarabe del valle*, with four pairs, and *La Bamba*, with ten dancers and eight men. In the latter, each girl is dressed differently and on a small ramp they form a fan. The men, dressed in white, are lined up on stage. One by one, the dancers enter and flirt with each other. As they dance, they choose their partners.

That's the end of the Mexican Show. Duration: twenty minutes. Date: November 1, 1958. Venue: International House. Four shows on the same night. I'll need the following: five Huichol hats and five "old-man" masks. Also, a typical Mexican white dress that's suitable for dancing. A copy of the record *La Bamba* performed by the Tlaliscoyan and Medellín bands (Peerless LPL 278) would be very helpful. I've written my parents to ask them for these things.

I went to a meeting at International House and I could tell that this year's competition for the World Dance Festival is going to be tough. Tomorrow I have classes in Labanotation and ballet. I hope my classmates don't leave me behind.

October 11

The photographer Harold Smith called me to say good-bye. I know that he wanted me to accompany him to the docks. Two inner forces struggled within me—Gloria the good woman and Gloria the dancer. The second won. Harold left at eleven in the morning, the same time as my ballet class, which I didn't want to miss.

October 12

My upbringing—which cultivated in me a hunger for knowledge, and a love of dance and books—separates me from some Americans. But, like most of them, to work without earning some money is unacceptable.

Today was an agreeable day. I took Labanotation, and then Madame Doubrovska's class. She's divine; I always feel strong and happy in her class. Her gaze infuses me with energy and her confidence in me is reassuring. I don't know if I'll ever dance well, but the important thing is that the effort to do so gives me a reason to live. If it weren't this, something else would be pushing me down this road. I'm tireless and nearly everything interests me. I'm happy when I dance, but also when I write or when I project my optimism onto another person.

October 15

A few weeks ago I picked up the violin, the dress, the box and the masks for old men. On one of my trips to the Ballet Theatre, I wore the dress for the first time. I've decided that I want dresses with low necklines and hemlines below the knee, made of common cloth with colored appliqués. In the ballet *La feria*, I'm playing the part of the young bride; I'll be able to do pirouettes and everything else. Today I couldn't make much headway with the choreography. I'm tired. The lead male dancer is awful and it's difficult to create for someone who isn't enthusiastic.

October 18

La feria is coming along and in only a week I've choreographed about half of it. But this requires so much effort that I'm nearly dead. I can't sleep at night because that's when I have my best ideas, and during the day I'm training, practicing the piano, studying for my classes, doing and teaching choreography, and rehearsing with amateurs for the *jarabes*. At least I'm in my element. I have my Labanotation class, which is wonderful. Well, *La feria* has to be completed in three more rehearsals.

October 19

The day is so beautiful it makes you feel close to God. Autumn is one of my favorite seasons; the colors take on a marvelous vivacity and variety. I'd never seen a red forest. The green is gone and in its place you find everything from yellow to purple. I feel happy because

I'm next to the sea and sky, and because I'm young and strong. I'm listening to Handel and Bach as I write and the Luke family opens shells. I feel so much that I can't express, the words get all mixed up and I can't describe my emotions.

My new ballet is turning out well. Despite the fact that it uses the same music as *Huapango*, it's completely different. *Huapango* is based on melodic themes, *La feria* on rhythm and harmony. The choreographic patterns are different and the steps are balletic but with a lot of character. In only four rehearsals I've created nearly all the choreography and my girls dance it well even though it still needs polishing.

I'm grateful to Balanchine and to the directors of this immense school, which I consider my home. Here, I learn more every day—perfecting my dance technique, studying the piano, creating choreography, reading. I pass the best hours of my day inside its walls. Everything is work, order and organization. Here I've found the maximum inspiration for my work. Last night I read the Lincoln Kirstein book, written in 1951. It explores the path of an imaginary young man who wants to become a choreographer. Now, in 1958 a young Mexican occupies the same place as Kirstein's character, but in much better conditions. The young "Alec" could never dance well and his choreographic works were solid but unoriginal—sad repetitions of Balanchine or Fokine (not my case).

October 23

My foot is a little better. As always, Doctor Henry Jordan, who's been giving me hydrotherapy, has been a great help. He thinks that Monday I'll be able to return to class.

Yesterday the masks arrived, along with the hats and the records. I'm not very satisfied with the choreography for the other *Huapango*. I don't know if it's because the girls are too tired or because the steps don't look good. Anyway, I'll have to go on without a male dancer. I have faith that in the final week before the performance, I'll find someone who'll resolve this problem. Carol Sumner learned my part yesterday; if I can't dance, she'll do it. Carol dances beautifully, but she's blond (not ideal for the part) and very classical. Nevertheless, in the last few rehearsals she's shown a lot of style and personality. In the *Jarabe pateño* I have a young girl named Karen Morell. She's short, with black hair down to her waist, immense black eyes, the whitest skin, and so graceful it's frightening. She moves with fluidity and elegance, acts well and knows how to flirt. She's also a solid dancer and a hard worker. She, Judy Friedman, and José Aruego will dance this *Jarabe* and I believe it will be a great success.

The other *Jarabe* is giving me gray hair. The young fellows are very agreeable, but they dance terribly. The girls don't look that good, either. I've included the parts of the five old men in the ballet. The dancers will be amateurs, but I hope they'll behave like professionals. The only solution to *La Bamba* is for me to dance it myself; I'm afraid that if I don't, it will be botched.

October 24

Today I finished *La feria*, which doesn't have a fair in it at all. With my tendency to create dance for the sake of dance, I left out the pantomime and the storyline, which gave the ballet a completely different flavor. The main reason for this was the absolute lack of male dancers. The entire ballet develops during the course of a single day in a small village. The girls dance continuously and I think it will be alright.

I've found a male dancer. He's a young black man who's not a great dancer but that doesn't bother me. I'll study the possibilities and invent movements which will make him look good. Doctor Jordan thinks that my foot is much better. Tomorrow I'll try to do barre. My numbers are looking better and the program is promising. The set designs are very pretty. It's time to go for my rehearsal at International House.

October 26

Yesterday I took barre and didn't feel bad, but after a long rehearsal my foot began to wage war again. The young man I found doesn't live up to my needs so I'll have to take him out of the program. But I have an idea how I can substitute his role. We rehearsed with the dresses and the blouses. Carol Sumner will wear my dress and take my role in the ballet. She looks beautiful in it and dances the part well. It will all be over in eight days. I don't plan to dance, but you never know what might happen. At any rate, the program will be a good one.

November 1

It's Sunday. The excitement is over and in its place I feel calm and happy. Over the last few weeks a multitude of problems has cropped up: my foot has improved, but I've developed problems with my ganglia, and have a cough and chest pains. Doctor Jordan sent me to one of his friends, who treated me effectively; within 24 hours my fever was gone. I went on working as if I were in the best of health.

The choreography went well and each day it's looking a little better. The boys came and practiced until midnight. The dancers learned the ballet, the pantomime, and the regional dances. The lights weren't ready, the music hadn't been taped, the costumes weren't ironed and a thousand other things still needed to be done. Roberto and José Aruego created the sets and completed them with the painter Tom Kendall. José was also the lead dancer in the program. He's a young man who identifies with words, rhythm, and grace. Roberto is an Italian with better bearing than the Spaniards of Carmen Amaya. There are only a few people I know who work that hard. Among the girls there were a couple who gave me problems, but I'm a little Hitler and I put them in their place right away. Even so, on the last day there were nervous upsets and hysterics, but I finally got everything under control. The sets were beautiful. Our backdrop was made from twenty-eight bedspreads the same color which we pieced together with pins. The dressing room was perfect, with two huge mirrors, a table for make-up and a long rack for all the costumes.

In the opening of the first program, Carol Sumner danced in my place. Frankly, despite her technique and grace, she wasn't able to establish a connection with the audience. The girls danced well but without spirit, and the applause was light. I felt that my ballet was a horrible failure. As soon as the applause had ended, José took off his mask and I entered with the black dress from Chiapas and we both began to dance the *Jarabe pateño*. We did it well and the audience warmed up a bit; after that came the *Jarabe del valle* with four pairs and later *La Bamba* with the voice and guitar of Pascual Navarro (on tape of course). It was impossible for them to dance to the other *La Bamba* recording since they couldn't follow the arbitrary changes in rhythm. This version of *La Bamba* was squishy and bad. There was little applause and I wanted to cry.

We got ready for the second program. After I'd injected some enthusiasm and energy into my young stars, everything was different. The house was full when I went out on stage and gave it my all. The audience became my strongest ally and the four numbers on the program received standing ovations. I was on stage for all the numbers except the *Jarabe pateño*, which was danced by Judy Friedman, Karen Morell, and José Aruego. *La Bamba* was as successful—or moreso—as when Pascual Navarro accompanied us. Continuous applause and shouts demanded an encore, but we couldn't go back on because everything was on tape.

The third program went as well as the second. Quite a few of my classmates attended the performance and were surprised. They called me "soloist," "ballerina," "star," a thousand names which I probably didn't deserve, but that certainly fed my ego. I had a group of thirty-one people and everyone helped to take down and fold up the set. I got home at five a.m., exhausted but happy. I gave all the participants a little something from Mexico.

November 2
I'm really thrilled about last Saturday. There was round applause from the audience every time I went onstage. The second and third concerts drew big audiences and were great successes. I felt repaid for all my efforts, illnesses, and setbacks. Everything is worth the effort when the audience responds so well.

As far as my foot, today I took class with Oboukhoff and it went well. I don't seem to have lost technique and my foot withstood the entire class. I've lost physical resistance, though; my entire body feels worn out. Today I went back to the nose-and-throat specialist. He thinks that before we consider operating for the chest pains, I must try to recover my energy; once I've recovered, I probably won't have to go under the knife. He made me promise to eat eggs for breakfast and meat for my other meals.

November 3
At last! I've been confirmed as an apprentice. I knew it since last Friday, but because I was told that six applicants had been selected and—as far as I knew—no one else had received notice, I couldn't count on it.

At the end of point class today, Barbara Horgan called on Carol Sumner and Patty McBride, a 15-year-old marvel who has a great future. Zoya is a Russian girl who's very pretty, vivacious and competent. Lili has a strong presence and a lot of style, and Susi, in my opinion, is also strong but isn't a good dancer. These are the five girls I'll be competing against for a full contract with the company. All of them are fifteen to nineteen years old, are slender and of optimum height, and have excellent technique. On hearing the news, they all burst into tears, laughing and hugging each other. Everyone in the school was watching and congratulated us. There were painful moments, like when I came face to face with the classmates who hadn't made it, and they congratulated me with eyes full of tears and faces painted with sadness. I couldn't cry or even laugh, but my hands shook when I wrote down the company's telephone number. When I went into the showers, I began to pray out loud in Spanish under the spray (I don't think anyone could hear me.): "Lord, be with me, grant me health, fortitude, intelligence, fluidity on stage, speed in rehearsals, the strength to continue fighting, the courage to triumph. Help me be what I must be." I stayed like that for a while, praying and crying as the water bathed me. I left feeling serene and ready to fight. I start tomorrow, from seven to ten at night.

Today I went to the rehearsal for *Medea*. The choreographer, Birgit Cullberg, is from Sweden. The music is by Béla Bartók. Medea's story is well established in dance and will have great emotional impact on the audience. The choreography is original and completely different from Balanchine's. I know it will be a success. Nevertheless, I find the dramatic movements of the soloists exaggerated in contrast to those of the corps de ballet, which are less expressive. It's a good ballet, but it wouldn't take much to turn it into a parody. Melissa Hayden is wonderful as Medea and her performance will be a great success. Allegra, as the Princess, is simply divine. Violette Verdy is also wonderful in this role, even though she interprets it in a different style. I spoke with the choreographer and congratulated her.

November 4

I got up early and went to study piano at the school. Violette Verdy, the company's new star, was there practicing. I was embarrassed because my piano exercises are very dull, but she was nice and not only told me that it didn't bother her, but actually began to hum the melody I was playing. This made me nervous and I made more mistakes than I should have. I took class with Vladimiroff and then with Doubrovska. I made an effort to dance well but didn't accomplish much.

November 6

Last night I went to the rehearsal for *Seven Deadly Sins*, which Balanchine is reviving. It was created in 1933 and premiered in Paris. Now it will be re-premiered in the coming season, which begins on the twenty-third of this month. It's an interesting ballet. I can't give a concrete opinion of it since I only saw it in-progress. It incorporates a lot of acting. The ballet technique in the piece is based on a free style. Also, a singer performs onstage, in mime; she doesn't dance. The characters include prostitutes and effeminate men. The music isn't that great, but it's appropriate. I went because the school hadn't responded with any news about my apprenticeship. As soon as I had the opportunity, I asked Janet when rehearsals would begin. She said either Thursday or Friday. The few words we exchanged left me feeling that nothing had changed in her plans and that I'll become an apprentice next season.

Of course, life plays the strangest tricks. I've been without work for two-and-a-half years, without the possibility of the tiniest offer and now, in the same week, I get three major ones: from Emily Frankel, the Ximenes-Vargas Company, and Balanchine. In the first two I would be a permanent member with the rank of soloist, but I'm choosing the most uncertain one—that of an apprentice with Balanchine's company. My main reason is that the New York City Ballet is the best company in the United States and one of the best in the world. It's also one of the most stable companies, and it stays in New York most of the time.

November 7

Today, the New York City Ballet took me on as an apprentice. I have a severe case of "athlete's foot," so this morning I put on my point shoes, went to the theater, and danced as well as I could. Balanchine watched the class and called me up afterwards. He made me take off my shoe and examined my left foot—the one I'd broken at the Fábregas Theater. He recommended that I use Freed shoes, that I always work in point shoes, and that I point my feet. He apologized for not attending my programs but didn't say anything about taking me into the company. Today I had two classes, the second with Nicholas Magallanes to rehearse the *adagio*; my partners were the best dancers in the company.

After class, Janet Reed, the ballet mistress, called me up and told me that the company is going to take on six girls as apprentices for *Symphony in C* and that I'm one of them. I'm the only one she told this to, perhaps thinking that rehearsals would begin on Sunday and that she didn't want me to rehearse with my group. This is what I've waited for and because I've worked so hard, it's made me fearless. Why? Because I don't belong to the company. An apprentice is not the same as a member. Everything depends upon how much they like my work, how quickly I learn, how I look and act on stage, how my health holds up, etc. I'll put everything into it so that my dancing meets Balanchine's standards, but I shouldn't forget that the company is taking on six apprentices, and perhaps only one of those will become a member.

November 8

I'll be leaving for the theater in half an hour. It's Sunday and I'm dancing with the City Center Ballet. Yesterday was difficult because, as usual, I was tested again. This time I didn't react as I should have. The company took on two ballerinas from the Ballet Theatre as permanent members. I found this out before class and it seemed so unfair that it was difficult for me to dance well. They were taken on because "they have experience," while I'm only considered worthy of the apprentice's role.

This morning I went to watch the matinee at City Center. *Seven Deadly Sins* premiered and Balanchine proved once again that he's the best and most versatile of choreographers. This isn't a ballet, but a musical drama which portrays the tragedy of a young woman who destroys her most noble sentiments in order to find a home. In the ballet, "Anna," played by Allegra Kent and Lotte Lenya, comes from the provinces seeking money to buy a house. The two figures represent the elements in conflict within her: Allegra plays the good side embodying art and spirit. Lotte plays the side that wants material things—and what money can buy. Lotte sings while Allegra dances; both are on stage throughout. It's moralistic and realistic, so much so it's disconcerting. The audience won't know what to expect when, instead of gazing at beautiful, spiritual "sylphs" they'll find themselves watching prostitutes, homosexuals, and every representation of vice. Allegra often appears practically nude and the corps de ballet presents a view of the elegant, refined cabaret, like in Paris or Hollywood, where clothing is replaced by gold dust. *Seven Deadly Sins* is a work representing a crude world, perfectly realized, with Allegra and Lotte as its protagonists. Allegra is a ballerina who can play the most beautiful swan or the crudest prostitute. Balanchine is a genius who, like Picasso, masters every style and surprises the audience with his versatility.

But, leaving the genius of Balanchine to one side for a moment, I'm certain that Gloria will also triumph in her career. It would be very convenient for her to enter the New York City Ballet because she would greatly expand her knowledge, but she has her own worth which must be recognized. Her goal isn't one but many-fold and her spirit is indomitable. Because of her strength and because she knows where her ideal lies, she isn't at the mercy of outsiders; she has her own creative force which impels her and gives her life.

November 11
Another day—six and a half hours—of continuous dancing, work, and satisfaction. I've been dancing more and more. My happiest day will be when I'm an inspiration for my companions. It doesn't matter that my feet are soaking in water; I know that the secret to staying optimistic is daily effort and believing that some day I'll be recognized, not only by the average person, like I am now, but by great figures in the dance world. Four years ago I had my first case of athlete's foot and there isn't a medicine that will get rid of it. I've always had sores between my toes, but when I dance I get so emotional that I don't notice the pain. Yesterday we had rehearsal in the theater and after running through *Symphony in C*, Janet Reed gave us a real point class. She also showed us some steps from various ballets in the repertoire, so the whole hour had the feeling of an audition. I did the best I could and, as always, I hope that some good will come from my efforts.

Today I went to Balanchine's house to take him some Christmas presents but he wasn't there and Tanaquil LeClercq never answers the door. I'd wrapped the little hand-painted white box in beautiful red paper for her. Inside I put one of the silver broaches. I'll give him the cuff links with the bull and matador. I sent Dr. Jordan the cuff-links shaped like horses. The basket earrings are for Judy Friedman and the handkerchief, for her mother. To my dear Thomas I sent $15—the earnings from one of our programs. I thought he could use it to have a good dinner and a fire on the eve of the twenty-fourth. I want to invite all my friends who live alone in New York for a good Christmas dinner.

Life magazine has published a wonderful article on *Seven Deadly Sins*. Balanchine is my eternal font of inspiration, the example that guides my life. Thanks to him, I've acquired the enormous amount of knowledge necessary for me to choreograph. He thinks I have choreographic talent, but he's also helped me see that my work was all basically composed "by ear."

November 16
Bizet's *Symphony in C* is a beautiful work. I remember that the first time I saw it, I wanted to dance it. Everything comes around and I believe that my turn has arrived. The rehearsal went well. We know

it almost perfectly: we learned it in one session. Thank God that Judy Friedman had already taught it to me. Miss Muriel Stuart, one of the teachers, said that Balanchine had told her he didn't think he was going to take any of us on as permanent members. This wasn't sweet news, but I'm not going to end my life over it. I know that I have a good future and that I will not only be a ballerina, but a choreographer and director of my own company.

November 18

I just got back from a rehearsal of *Concerto Barroco*, which I attended as a spectator. It's set to Bach and the choreography rivals the music in its beauty and depth. Allegra Kent and Violette Verdy are the soloists. The former, as usual, has a harmonious style and is delightful to watch. Violette has a lot of personality and is a very good ballerina, but she's going through hell because she still doesn't know the piece. During the rehearsals she concentrates and is respectful to the choreographers and amiable with her companions, without talking down to the girls in the corps de ballet. At the end of the rehearsal I went up to Balanchine and told him my opinion of *Concerto Barroco*, that it's profoundly religious. I know that he liked the idea because his eyes shone and a subtle smile passed across his face. But his answer was "Allegra is divine!"

The previous rehearsal was for *Souvenirs*, by Todd Bolender. I enjoyed watching Janet Reed return to the stage. She's the ballet mistress of the company, but I believe she hadn't danced in public since the birth of her child. She's redheaded, freckled, short and thin, and has great talent. She's not only a good ballerina but a great actress. She always dances her roles to perfection. In my opinion, Janet is one of the reasons why ballet has reached a superior level in the United States. When you go to the Sadler's Wells Ballet or the Royal Ballet, you certainly see technical perfection and optimum plasticity, but no personality, or any true talent, for that matter, and no twentieth-century pieces. Janet is impregnated with life and projects it through her dancing.

I took two very good classes today and gave my best effort. I know that I've progressed, but I also know that I need to improve a thousand-fold. I have style and personality, even though I need to purify my technique. It's a never-ending task, but that doesn't scare me. Sonia Castañeda and Jorge Cano watched Madame Doubrovska's point class and I think they enjoyed it. I danced on point shoes so soft that they seemed not to be there. I should buy a tape recorder but I think it would be better for me to purchase three or four pairs of point shoes and pay the doctor who treated me when I had problems with my ganglia. I need a tape recorder, but it'll have to wait; I simply don't have time for my group during my apprenticeship with the New York City Ballet.

I spoke with an agent who saw my group perform last Sunday and is interested in working with me. Everything happens at once and you just have to refuse some offers. My athlete's foot is better, but it hasn't been cured. My eyelids feel like paper—the skin is dry, wrinkled, and scaly. When I wake up I look like I'm seventy years old. Maybe it's because my nerves are making me sweat too much or because I've lost some weight. Otherwise I'm strong and well. It feels just like home here. I think that the multicebrine vitamins are helping me. My first performance with the New York City Ballet is just a few days away, next Tuesday, November 25. It begins at eight-thirty and ends at eleven. Good luck, partner!

November 20
Today I took two classes and because I'd decided to improve my feet, it meant double the work. Every muscle is a pinprick, every bone a pain. I studied the piano for an hour-and-a-half, and even though it seems impossible, it helped relax me. We haven't rehearsed again. Next Tuesday we're having our debut and we haven't tried on our costumes, familiarized ourselves with the ballet or rehearsed with the orchestra. I hope that my mind stays calm and that I can perform well.

November 23
My uncle Emilio Calderón Puig gave me two tickets to the Mexican National Symphony, which was performing at Carnegie Hall. The concert consisted of Revueltas's *Sensemayá*; Moncayo's *Huapango*, Chávez's *Indian Symphony* and Shostakovitch's *Fifth*. The house was packed and the concert was good. I didn't go backstage to congratulate them, which I regret, but I was too tired.

Despite the fact that it was Sunday, I worked, though it wasn't very productive ... At ten we had class on stage at City Center with all of the members of the New York City Ballet. Janet Reed's class is very difficult; it reminds me of Madame Dambré's in some respects. After that we had rehearsal from eleven until two in the afternoon with Balanchine. We went through the entire *Symphony in C* by Bizet. My part is near the end so I have to wait through four movements before going out on stage; with my constant preoccupation about how well I'll perform, it's a little tough. We went through it quickly and they gave us "newcomers" as little attention as they did the "old-timers" who could perform the ballet in their sleep. They don't waste time on teaching you here. If you do it, that's fine. If you don't, you're out! I think that despite the fact that I made a few mistakes, I wasn't all that bad.

Afterwards I stayed to watch the other rehearsals until seven at night. Sitting passively without being able to learn, dance, or direct really wears me out. If I ever make it into the company, it's going to be hard for me to be part of the corps de ballet. The truth is that, in my position, I ought to plead with God to let me into the corps. But I know that it would take work for me to get used to it. I've watched Violette Verdy, Barbara Walzak, Patricia Wilde, Melissa Hayden, Diana Adams, and Allegra Kent, and as usual, despite the fact that each has talent, Allegra wins the prize. She dances fluidly and her source of energy is almost magical. Some of the girls in the corps are as good as, or better, than Ana Cardús. When I watch them work, I realize that the company isn't just any set of dancers assembled intelligently; it's the best in the world. Balanchine has united elements of every nationality.

November 24
Tomorrow I'll be dancing and I'll earn $15 in my first performance with the New York City Ballet. Today I tried on the tutu that I'll use, the one that Melissa Hayden used last season. I hope I do it justice.

November 26
For the first time, a New York City Ballet program included our names. I danced in Melissa Hayden's tutu and even though I'm sure it wasn't the same experience for the audience, I knew how to carry it off. My nerves weren't terribly under control, but there's no doubt that I'm a veteran of the stage. Balanchine and my friends congratulated us.

November 27
Everything went well. After waiting for two hours, it was my turn. The members of the company arrived one by one and wished me luck. I danced well, but I could have done better. I was very nervous and when I smiled, my lips trembled from the effort. I didn't make

any big mistakes and the rough spots were difficult to notice. Last night God was with me. Afterwards I approached Balanchine, who told me that I'd done well, as had my five comrades. Judy Friedman gave me a bouquet of roses.

November 28
Today, Friday, will be my second performance. This morning I took class with Oboukhoff; afterwards I rehearsed and worked on point for two hours. I just now finished closing Tom's piano. He's my neighbor and he lets me come in to practice when he and Steve aren't at home. I'm very tired, but I hope to dance well. All that should concern me is staying calm; once you've conquered your nerves there's no danger. I've received the photos from the program at International House. Yesterday was Thanksgiving, one of the few days when everything shuts down in the States. I couldn't take class so I used the time to write, read, wash and sew my tights.

November 29
Last evening I danced for the second time. I was very tired, but I'm always tired, so that's normal. I made myself up in fifteen minutes, put on my tights, and went down to the wings. The first ballet was *Interplay* by Jerome Robbins, and I liked it so much that I hope to be able to dance it some day. The company has prepared it very well. The second ballet, *Orpheus*, by Balanchine and Stravinsky, is very beautiful, even though the choreography becomes monotonous in some places because it's so slow and simple. Nevertheless, it contains important artistic innovations. Diana Adams is a great ballerina. Her *Eurydice* is perfect. Nicholas Magallanes is a great actor, even if he's not strictly a dancer. He's handsome and develops his role successfully. *Still Point* (Bolender-Debussy) was the best of the evening. I always thought of Melissa Hayden as a great virtuoso, but last night I saw her as an artist. Her interpretation was so true and profound that I was filled with admiration. As I watched her, I understood what distinguishes a soloist from the corps de ballet.

We dancers in the corps are painted-up marionettes. The expression on our faces is false. Our nerves destroy our technique and we smile because Balanchine wants us to smile. We are told to count and to keep our minds on technique, which results in a lamentable interpretation. What's most important is that I've been an artist. In my own group I've danced at the level of a Melissa, without her potent technique, but by submitting completely to my art. For this reason, dancing with the New York City Ballet hasn't given me any joy. I suppose it's because I haven't really danced with the company. I've counted, played the role of a doll and raised my legs, just like or worse than the coolest of my companions. I know that it's much more difficult to be an artist than to be a member of the corps. You develop a kind of complex among 48 dolls moving in unison. But I've got a brain and I know my point of attack. First, I need to develop control over my nerves and second, I need to feel the joy of dancing and share that with my audience. When this happens, my smile will be complete and I'll be satisfied. I've received my paycheck.

November 30

I'm very happy to be Gloria and to have so many interests. I don't think I'll ever have time to be bored. As far as my first impressions as an "almost-member" of the New York City Ballet, I'd say that I knew beforehand that it wouldn't completely satisfy me unless it opened a path for me to become a soloist. When I do achieve my goal, then I'll be able to dance my true self, without the limitations of patterns or lines. If I'm accepted, I think I'll gain experience, connections, etc. I'll stick with it a few years and after that, if I find that dancing with my own group is more satisfying, then I'll throw myself full-time into finding a good manager to tour the world, not as a gypsy, but as a Mexican. I've found a place where I can give myself completely to an audience. I know that even if I have to wait one or two years, it won't be a lost cause because I carry my ideal within me and I can perform onstage any moment I choose. If I am taken into the company, I'll try by every means to continue my musical education and my choreographic experiments.

December 8

I danced in the theater last night and felt sad because my part was so small that I couldn't give anything to the audience. I just smiled and danced a few steps, but inside I was inert. I can't even say that I danced perfectly. I only have a few steps and they're not very well-executed. I watched the rest of the program and I liked *Medea* by Birgit Cullberg more than ever. Each time I see it I'm ready to absorb more of it. It's the reverse with *Agon*. The more I see it the less susceptible I am to its message. *Serenade* is Balanchine's ballet set to the music of Tchaikovsky. In my opinion, it's one of the jewels of choreography.

December 12

Today I went to the home of Violette Verdy, the great French dancer who is now the star of the New York City Ballet. Her mother is very intelligent and knows a lot about music, but that's not all. She thinks she can understand the composer through his sound. I am most interested in setting a ballet to Chávez's *Fifth Symphony*. Violette, her mother and I listened to it several times. They didn't know it but were fascinated by it. Mrs. Verdy thought that it suggested first the mildness of youth and then social conflict, finishing with a battle between the old and the new in civilization.

This gave me the idea of doing a ballet with the symbol of Malinche, who would represent the clash of two civilizations, the conflict of belonging to one race by blood and another by belief, spirit, and love. I would trace her life from her royal origins to her sale into slavery and her encounter with Cortés, who took her into the Christian religion and became her man. All of this would well serve a ballet and the music of Chávez would be a wonderful score for it. Madame Verdy agreed. But I need to study and I can't rush it. You can't commit errors with history. First, I should write out the historical features that are relevant to La Malinche. Then I should put this history into scenes, in accordance with the music, and only when the path is clear, when the music and the story are knitted into one, should I begin to create a language that tells everything through dance. Without words, only with movement.

December 17

I had a good day today because I danced better than usual. My teachers congratulated me on several occasions. I know that if it were up to them, I would have entered the New York City Ballet a long time ago. I know that I'm not going to enter this season, which ends the first week of February and will be in recess until July. Another year of effort, but it hasn't been badly spent. I'm dancing better, but I have a lot of ground to cover. I worked on *Huapango* between my two classes and I'm happy with my new girl: Alejandra Vernon. She's fourteen years old, tall and slim, with a very pretty line. As a dancer, she's potent and elegant.

December 21

Last night I danced in City Center and I made a huge mistake. Some dancers who were talking offstage distracted me and I missed one of my steps. I don't think anyone noticed, but it's enough that *I* know

I did. I'm very bored with *Symphony in C* and I don't know whether being a full member of the company would make any difference. I wasn't born to be part of the corps. All of us feel small and inept alongside Balanchine. Even my own choreographic production has been put aside because I can't work with complete self-assurance. I'm working day by day simply to master the technical ability necessary to have a stage at my disposal. Last night Vicky Simon hurt her arm badly. She danced and cried at the same time. I know the second movement of *Symphony in C* because Judy Friedman taught it to me. Janet Reed knows it too and she stepped in even though I could have replaced Vicky. The doctor came to see her and said that she shouldn't dance, so they need a substitute, but the day's gone by and the telephone still hasn't rung.

December 26

Today is Christmas and my ex-ballerinas—Marlene Mesavage, Judy Friedman, and Joysanne Sidimus—came over for a couple of hours. They're working in the television studios because they're going to dance the *Nutcracker* at nine-thirty at night and they're using their afternoon to eat and spend time with me. Marlene is making money now and has become a real icon. She dresses exquisitely and is becoming more beautiful by the minute. Esther Villavicencio, the Cuban ballerina now with the Chicago Ballet, also came. The *Nutcracker* came off well. Balanchine played Herr Droselmeyer and his acting was wonderful.

December 31

A few days ago the Ximenes-Vargas Spanish company called me again. They need a female dancer who has classical technique and is Spanish (or at least, Spanish-looking) and they think that I fit the bill. I'd be doing my numbers as a soloist and receive Flamenco lessons from the best Spanish company. I don't know what to do because, even if I've got one foot in Balanchine's company, I'm not in it yet. Furthermore, they won't take me until September, at the earliest. But if I leave now, it would be like refusing to join the company. I've fought for two years and I think that I'm closer than ever to being selected. There are several issues confusing me. On the one hand I know that I want to fight, no matter how long it takes, to gain a good position in the best company in the world—the New York City Ballet. But I know that if I ever become a member, I'd be very unhappy in the corps. I was born to be the head, not the tail, and I want to be the head of a lion, not a rat. I've got so much ambition; it doesn't matter how big the obstacles are, I am sure I can overcome them. I know that I'm dancing better than before and that I'll continue to make progress.

On the other hand, I should be realistic and understand that I'm a dreamer. If I have the opportunity to take a good position with a company, I shouldn't refuse it. But no, I know what I want and that is to be a ballerina and a choreographer. I know that I should learn music and that I must continue choreographing. So, forget Ximenes-Vargas. I'll continue working without averting my gaze from my goal. Today, the last day of 1958, I find myself tired, tired because of my two classes, two hours of choreography, three of piano and various household chores. I know that 1959 will be just as difficult as or worse than it's always been. But I'm not afraid of the fight. I'm happy and look toward the future with optimism and confidence.

1959

January 2

Today I took two good classes—one of them the *adagio* taught by Nicholas Magallanes. I used to be very bad at dancing with a partner. I remember that when my sister Margara was here, I took *adagio* with Caton, at the Ballet Russe; I was truly pained that my little sister had to watch me. Now I'm the best in the class. I have a lot of strength in my back, my points aren't beautiful but they're strong, and it's a marvelous class. I rehearsed *Huapango* for two hours. I'm redoing the choreography. I know it's more intellectual than the original. It's losing its spontaneity and gaining variety and interest. I spent yesterday cleaning house. I would have liked to see in the New Year by visiting a good museum, but I took advantage of the fact that I wasn't very tired to wash walls, floors, windows, etc.

January 6

I've struggled my entire life to be a classical dancer. God has tested me in every way and it might seem as if He's tried to keep me from my goal. I began late and with a bad teacher. I lost two precious years and by the time I was thirteen, when I studied with Nelsy Dambré, I had to fight not only to learn but also to destroy the vices and defects I'd acquired. From then on, each year was "adorned" with falls, sprained ankles, pulled tendons and inactivity. What I gained in six months was lost in the following six. Despite everything, I was able to develop some power which, along with fluid movement, good posture and natural style, allowed me to distinguish myself. When I was in my best condition, I made the mistake of going to Canada where I failed to acquire a technique, and also became weaker and suffered emotional shocks that almost made me hate dance. I became a little unstable mentally and began succumbing to absurd deviations in my diet and bad influences. Thanks to my character, I was able to conquer myself, and against all obstacles, arrived in New York to begin again.

I've struggled here for two years. The insignificant Mexican ant has grown. She is now known in the dance world, not only as one of the best dancers in The School of American Ballet, but also as a choreographer and director. I'm the favorite of my teachers and am protected by Balanchine, the best choreographer in the world. In addition to not paying a cent for my dance classes, I have permission to use the members of the advanced classes for my own professional purposes, to use the salons and the record players, and to practice the piano. I'm the only person who is allowed to watch all the rehearsals and performances. I'd be a fool to give up now. I must continue struggling, and if I'm indeed a better dancer than before, I still have a thousand details to improve. What's important is improving and gaining knowledge; fame and public recognition will come later. I know I can achieve success when I desire it through my Mexican group. So I must continue choreographing and studying music and dance, at least for one or two more years. My group will continue as before. We'll dance when and where we have the opportunity. In fact, we may have the chance to go to Puerto Rico to perform, subsidized by International House.

January 12

I received my parents' Christmas gift. I explained to them that they didn't need to continue sending me money, that Lou earns enough and with the scholarship from Balanchine, we're in the black. On the other hand, I added, it *would* be very useful because I've decided to buy myself a piano. I absolutely must study music and without an instrument it's hard to keep up with my lessons. I don't know what I'd give to have a day with more hours and a more resilient body. I know that I must learn to read music, even to create my own rhythms, but I don't have the time to study at a good school like Julliard.

I've been doing choreographic experiments using simple beats. But the only thing that occurs to me is to do a series of movements in four. I've set hand gestures in counterpoint with the rest of the body and then I've moved the dancers in the style of a fugue. With four bars, the first two are used as the primary counts and the third as the conclusion. I'm doing this to explore and develop my imagination. One thing that worries me is that I live so isolated from the musical and literary movements of our day that I hardly have material to work with. I feel as if I'm on an island inhabited only by people worried about physical training. My radio's broken and my free time is so limited that I haven't been able to have it fixed.

Today I went to a cocktail party at the New York Library that marked the opening of an exhibit on the history of the New York City Ballet. All the prominent figures of the ballet world, except for Balanchine, were there. I went with Lou, Kenneth Dewey, and

Graciela de Majo. I was invited because Kenneth's mother organized the show. I was very sociable and it's worth mentioning that even though I'm a foreigner, I knew more guests than anyone else there. The company's dancers, many of whom have been here for 20 years, passed almost unnoticed.

January 15

Last night I was sitting in my dressing room finishing putting on my make-up when the door opened and in walked Janet Reed. She had something in her look that made me tremble. "Lila Popper is sick, Gloria. Could you go on for her?" Without even knowing which ballet she was referring to, I replied in the affirmative with complete calmness. Only my hand shook a little and felt cold. In a few minutes the dancers who were performing the second movement of *Symphony in C* came up and taught it to me in the space of ten minutes. When they left, I realized that this was an opportunity to either show my abilities or watch the doors of the company swing shut. I concentrated as well as I could and begged God to allow me to keep calm. If I lost my head I'd be defeated, but if I didn't, I'd earn a point in my favor. It was the night of a premiere. *Native Dancer*, with music by Vittorio Rieti and choreography by Balanchine, would be danced for the first time and the hall was full of celebrities. When my turn came, I felt immensely happy. I went out on stage and danced with all my soul and with absolute perfection. I didn't make a single mistake. The entire company was in the wings watching me: Balanchine, Janet Reed, Lincoln Kirsten, and everybody else. At the end, everyone congratulated me, including Balanchine. You can't imagine how satisfied and happy I felt! There isn't any pay quite like it.

This morning Balanchine brought a little package to school for me. It was a Christmas gift, a beautiful little German box with a very fine perfume inside. But my day has been difficult. I've discovered that I don't have any "turn out" to speak of. The foot that got fractured at the Fábregas Theater has gotten worse. I turn it and I don't use all of the metatarsals when I put weight on it. I tried to do everything cleanly while I was at the barre, but when it came to the *adagio* I was completely worn out. They're very delicate muscles and I need to watch myself. It will take at least a year to correct this but if I get desperate and try to achieve everything too quickly, then I'm going to start out with damaged tendons.

January 18

Symphony in C was canceled last night because the company is so overworked that several of the soloists are out, mainly with damaged tendons and slipped knees. This made me sad, but I was tired, too. Today, Sunday, I'll dance in the evening program. Last week was especially hard because I decided to correct the weakness in my foot that I recently discovered: I fought against my own body so much that every class was exhausting.

Today's *New York Times* ran an absolutely masterful article by John Martin on *Seven Deadly Sins*. I felt so mediocre when I compared his article with mine that I don't know if I should publish it. John Martin describes and criticizes *Seven Deadly Sins* with such precision, that if someone reading his commentary hasn't seen it, he or she can appreciate the full value of the work of Balanchine, Kurt Weill, and Bertolt Brecht.

Speaking of the final scene, my first impression was erroneous. It has nothing to do with an elegant cabaret. The scene recalls German art films from the early thirties. The stage is set to look like a movie studio which is populated with masked characters that symbolize self-centered people. The text portrays the character Anna as a realist who preaches the most immoral codes from a pulpit. Her speech goes like this: "Fight for success, comfort, posterity . . . life is short, youth grows old. Obtain the highest price for your love while you still have beauty, etc." The beautiful Anna is envious of these beautiful beings that enjoy liberty and the fruits of their sins. She renounces all her moral principles after she is taunted by her family, who ask God to show their daughter not the road to posterity, but to prosperity and who, on opening each letter from Anna, search for money inside to build a house in Louisiana. The family appears in the background throughout the entire work. They are represented by four male singers—two sons, a father and a mother (with a bass voice)—all of whom express their happiness at seeing Anna earn money at the cost of her honor and who go on building their seven-floor house, their seven cities, their seven sins. Kurt Weill wrote the music, Bertolt Brecht the text, and Balanchine choreographed it. It's a moral work and excellent theater.

January 21

If someday I become a permanent member of Balanchine's company, I'll earn $120 a week, part of which will go to cover my costs; another part will go into the bank, and the rest will be for my parents. I promise this, and I keep my promises.

January 22

Last night I went to visit Marlene Mesavage. The poor thing is in the hospital. Six days ago she had an epileptic attack and since then she's been in the neurology ward. They're giving her all of the tests to determine the cause. I think it's simply exhaustion, and excessive nervous tension. Nearly all of the dancers are ill. There are thirteen out sick. Ballet is the most demanding of professions. These girls are dancing for a year, every night, learning new roles, rehearsing from five to eight hours a day, performing and dieting. The nervous tension this creates is indescribable. You have to have nerves of steel. I hope that Marlene gets better soon. I brought her a book by Anton Chekhov. She's the dancer who has given me the best photos for a book on Mexican ballet. I created the biggest part in *Huapango* for her.

At the ballet I ran into Billy Sandberg, Sweden's leading dancer. After the performance we went out for coffee and cake and we stayed out talking until quite late. He's a very intelligent man and one of the few people I've encountered in New York whose conversation fascinates me because, when we're together, it's not me, but him doing the talking, explaining and criticizing. With each of his ideas he gives me a little lesson and reveals something that I've been incapable of discovering for myself. His view of art is so connected to his outlook on life that they've become one. He's made me see that I run a great risk by closing myself up in Balanchine's circle. I need to be myself and must live intensely, learning how to create without books, techniques and closed studios. He suggested that I look out onto the world, which is full of misery and calamity, and allow myself to feel the presence of God. I don't want to become one of those "pretend" artists who talk a lot and say nothing of real value. When I look at my choreographic work, I don't know if it has a true message or if it's simply a product of my vanity.

January 27

Tomorrow my piano course ends and I'll have to perform for the directors of the school. My teacher is a good person. Yesterday I read one of Beethoven's sonatas so I could practice reading scores. The Concerto was tape-recorded and my teacher had the score. I got lost in a few parts, but I could pair the sounds and notes in some places. I'm very tired and, to top it off, I've got the beginning of a cold—my glands are swollen and I've got a cough. I'm working a lot, but I don't regret it. Today I danced from eleven to four-thirty in the afternoon. I've significantly corrected my weak turn-out so that, hopefully, it won't be an issue of years, only months.

My choreographic work gets me so enthusiastic that I can't sleep. For hours and hours I do nothing more than think of sculptural figures and musical sounds. About Felipe Segura, I know that my work with the Mexicans won't produce a red cent, but it's useful for me to confront the audience as a choreographer and a soloist. It would also be good for me to appear as a guest artist there, to go to Mexico and dance in such a large theater. I hope that the instruction I've received since I left my homeland will allow me to work with the Mexican group and preserve some harmony. I think I've made enough progress in my understanding of human beings and that I'll be able to face my old enemies with due calm.

January 31

Yesterday was an important day. Mrs. Nancy Lassalle, coordinator for the Ballet Society of the New York City Ballet, came to the school at twelve-thirty to see *Huapango*. She seemed very interested in me and this will possibly result in some help for the creation of a workshop that would make people available so I can create new ballets.

At night we had a performance and I did well. My name now appears in two places because I'm recognized in the credits for the second movement of Bizet's *Symphony in C*, replacing Ruth Sobotka. It was a very tough day because I had two difficult classes, three hours of rehearsal and later a performance until eleven-thirty at night. At night I continued dancing in my dreams and my aching body prevented me from sleeping well.

Today I had a very good class. Tomorrow will be the last performance. I don't know if that's only for the season or forever. I know that my principal enemy is my vocation for choreography and that both Balanchine and Nancy Lassalle see me as a future choreographer, which prevents them from seeing my qualities as an interpretive artist.

February 12

Last night after the rehearsal we all got together with Tom Kendall and Peter Dickinson, respectively, a painter and a musician. Peter is a young English composer who has a scholarship at Julliard. His music is played often. He had several spools of tape recordings and we listened to a concerto for strings and a suite of eight variations for piano.* It's very modern and complicated. His work seems completely cerebral to me; the music doesn't move me, but because it's interesting, I think we can work together. Next week, we're getting together to tape some of his works for ballet and I'll select something that serves my purpose to create a *pas de trois* for two men and a woman. Or maybe I'll do a composition on his eight variations for piano. Anyway, once the first stage is completed I'll have a clearer notion of the dance movements suggested by the strange combinations of sounds and rhythms. After that, we'd like to do a ballet based on the same idea.

I met Peter Dickinson during the day. If everything goes well, *Huapango* will be danced today in Mexico. How I'd like to be there! For some reason or other God sees to it that our desires aren't always fulfilled. This way Margara will have the opportunity to dance my ballet in a role that will confirm her talent.

February 15
Yesterday I received my father's telegram informing me of the success of Margarita Contreras and the other dancers in *Huapango* at Bellas Artes. I was happy and grateful. I know they're performing it again in the auditorium today. I'm a little worried about the size of the theater and the orchestra conductor, but I'm certain that everything will turn out. I also received letters and reviews. These pleased me, especially the one on *El mercado,* because it had a useful critique. The reviewer says that the mime scene is anemic, but I don't think that the rest of the work, from that point on, lacks energy. Our lungs prove that there's a lot of dancing at the end!

February 16
Today I actually finished the class. My foot is still infected but it looks as if the wound is starting to heal. Balanchine came into the studio and I greeted him with a smile. The class for the ten selected dancers began. Madame Doubrovska gave the class and Balanchine watched. I think that the new members of the company will come from their ranks. Even though it seems incredible, I've accepted this with absolute calm. He knows me, he knows my work, he recommends me, but nevertheless he doesn't have space for me in his company. My life goes on, and will go on, always forward.

---

* Dickinson's *Suite of Eight Variations for Piano* is the musical score from which Contreras developed the choreography for *Vitálitas.*

In the morning, I saw Nancy Lassalle, the coordinator of the Friends of City Center Ballet Society. She saw *Huapango* in rehearsal and asked me what I was going to do during the summer. She'll be calling me tomorrow or the next day and maybe we'll reach some agreement on a job where I'll be able to do the choreography with her supporting the dancers necessary for new works. I hope to hear from Mexico about the concluding concerts of *Huapango*.

March 6
I haven't been to see "The Chiefs": Kirstein, Balanchine, Betty Cage, etc. I think that when I do I should carry a folder with programs, photos and reviews of my work in Mexico along with me. I asked my parents to send me these as quickly as possible—including photos of Anita Cardús, Jorge Cano, Silvia Domínguez, Cora Flores, Margarita Contreras or me rehearsing or performing. I reminded them that the fellow from *Hoy* magazine, who in the past had taken photos of me arriving at the airport, took a lot of photos both before and after the premiere of *Huapango*.

March 17
I received a letter from my dear sister Margara. It contains the joy and youth of a fifteen-year-old artist. In it I can see why the theater is an eternal lover: once you know it in depth, it's impossible to leave it. The applause, the intoxication of the rhythm, the emotion of movement, all of this is theater. I love Margara and am very proud of her. I knew from the time she was three years old that she'd be successful and that's why I worked to give her what I didn't have: knowledge of English and music, and a strong foundation in dance. I'm hoping that she now focuses on her technique, and that she realizes the value of this sacrifice for dance in terms of her future as an artist. *Huapango* certainly marks the beginning of a great career for her. Congratulations and thank you, Margarita, for ensuring that my ballet was a success.

March 24
Today was a day full of bustle. After class, I went to City Center to talk with Nancy Lassalle, the coordinator of the company. She gave me some strong advice, but her ideas aren't nonsense. She thinks that study ought to be my first objective. She wants me to study with Martha Graham during the summer so that I learn her style of modern dance. Balanchine thinks that Graham is one of the few

valuable contributors to modern dance. She also wants me to take more music lessons and to read poetry. "Pictorial movement is also important, but don't think about taking musical theater." I told her about *Huapango* and its success, which included fourteen curtain calls. I showed her the photos and reviews, perfectly presented in a new scrapbook the size of *Hoy* magazine. "The most important thing is for you to learn your technique to create choreography, not with the hope that some day they'll be in the repertoire of the New York City Ballet, but simply to develop yourself." They've decided to pay a pianist and to form a group that will work under my direction and I'll be responsible for creating one ballet a month. That's all there is to it. They'll also try to get me a scholarship with Martha Graham and at the school of music. This evening she called me to invite me to her home on Wednesday evening to meet the Mexican poet Elena Paz Garro. I do regret not knowing anything about Mexican poetry of our time. All in all, the Balanchine policy is to make you feel insignificant and immature, to force you to work, to study, to progress. I know what I've got to deal with and I accept that. You can only achieve excellence through intense effort and I know that if they didn't think I have talent they wouldn't worry about my future.

March 25

Last night I got out of rehearsal at eight-thirty. Nancy Lassalle invited me to her house to meet the Mexican poet Elena Garro, the former wife of Octavio Paz. The Lassalles' house suggests wealth. It isn't an apartment, but a real house several stories high. All the walls are covered with modern art. In the living room, instead of a table, they have an old Spanish chest, pre-Hispanic clay figurines, and modern art objects from all over the world. The decor speaks to their excellent taste, extravagance, and wealth.

The Mexican actor Carlos Navarro was there and we began the party in the most original manner you can imagine. He was talking about the Ballet Concierto, saying that ballet in Mexico was better than theater, that *Swan Lake* had been marvelous, and so on. He'd also seen *Tragedy in Calabria* and *Huapango*. When he got to that, I asked him what he thought of it and he said: "It's the worst thing I've ever seen in my life. It's an insult to the music. It has no reason to exist." He went on like this to such an extreme that I think he would have swallowed me whole had I given him a few seconds more. I smiled and said, "You're speaking to the choreographer."

What excuses! The poor man nearly fainted. Instead, he turned pale, then red as a tomato: "In reality, the choreography was divine," he stuttered, "in fact, much too good for Moncayo. More worthy of Mozart, I would say. Yes, that's it. Mozart." Oh well, Carlos just passed through one of the most embarrassing moments of his life. I think he simply missed the sombreros, the drunks and the typical bottle of tequila. I teased him for a while and won him over in the old Mexican macho style. It goes without saying that by the time he left the house that evening, I'd conquered him. I took it very well and am proud of how well I handled the situation in front of a future "patron."

At about ten that night Elena Paz made her entrance. She's short, friendly, frank, and intelligent. She's a woman of the world, more Parisian than Mexican. She can't stand Mexicans. I suppose that she couldn't adapt to our atmosphere, so full of prejudice and hypocrisy that talent is simply unable to triumph. Those who don't have it make sure that anyone who does gets strangled quickly. She knows of the so-called talents that shamefully invade every branch and leaf of our Mexico. We were together until two in the morning and arranged to see each other next week.

April 2

Balanchine came in to watch the morning class. I felt badly about that because I didn't feel well and I didn't dance half as well as when I'm in good health. But anyway, I know that he'll never take me into his company. Maybe he's right and it would be better if I devoted all of my time to choreography. But even if this sounds logical, it doesn't really make me happy. I want to dance, too. New York is still trapped in winter. We've had snow, rain, fog, and cold temperatures. One gets used to living among grays and I think that it doesn't affect my mood as much as it once did.

The Bolshoi Ballet will be coming soon, at the cost of $15 a seat. Despite the price, I want to go. From what I've heard, it's a marvelous company but I want to judge it through my own eyes. I would go several times but doubt that I can at that price. I hope the play I'm working on closes soon; if it doesn't, I'll give my notice because I see no reason to be in it. It's a waste of time and isn't benefiting me at all.

April 6

It looks like Balanchine will use me as an apprentice. I bumped into him yesterday and, steeling myself with courage, I went directly to the point: I asked him why he hadn't given me a contract and explained to him that although my principal goal in life was choreography, dance, as an interpretive art, made me immensely happy. I asked him if he thought that this was simply vanity on my part. I expressed my desire to have a stage to work from, and I also explained that it's in dance where I find my greatest strength and that I'm now discovering new movements, gestures, and plastic forms. To my surprise, he approved of everything I said and couldn't hide his satisfaction. "That's the way I think, too," he said. He explained that the reason he hadn't taken me was because he knows that I can give a lot more, that he demanded perfection of me and that I still haven't achieved it. He used the example of Nora Kaye, the prima ballerina of the Ballet Theatre. In his opinion, she has nothing. Her body, her face, her technique, everything runs against the rhythm of ballet. Nevertheless, Nora has become an international figure in the dance world. She exemplifies ambition and work. "And if Nora could, why can't you? Even her nose is artificial. You, on the other hand, are perfectly proportioned, with the exception of your calves, which are a little small. Work should be your motto."

He explained why it was necessary for me to be both physically and mentally superior. He wants me to be better than the best dancers of the company because that is the only way to create choreography for them, without being influenced by them or achieving below their level. Rather, I should raise them to my level and open new paths for them through dance. He compared himself to me and encouraged me to work more every day.

It looks like I've left a positive impression on Tamara Geva too: having heard about Balanchine's recommendation that I study modern dance with Martha Graham during the summer, she's been trying to get me a scholarship. Tamara went to see Martha Graham and arranged an appointment for Thursday at four in the afternoon.

My next choreographed piece will be based on music by the Englishman Peter Dickinson, a contemporary composer and friend. First I'll use his *Eight Piano Pieces*, a work that lasts about thirteen minutes. It's completely cerebral and will most likely challenge my sense of spontaneity. The meter is totally arbitrary and I'll have to use more head than heart.

April 10

I just left Martha Graham, the greatest choreographer of modern dance. I'm convinced that in Balanchine's opinion, she's as important to modern dance as he is to classical ballet; of course, he doesn't say this, but I know he thinks so. I believe she was impressed by my work. We spoke for half-an-hour. She was enveloped in a huge black oriental-style jacket. Martha Graham is very elegant and has a dignified and intelligent face. She's about sixty, but looks a lot younger. At first, our conversation was a little cool, but as I spoke and explained my ideas about movement, her expression changed and a deeply interested and pleasant look emerged on her face. She browsed through my two books and at the end gave me so much praise that I felt uncomfortable. She congratulated me for being independent, for having ambition, and for working to fulfill my dreams. She arranged for me to call her next Monday. She wants me to watch one of her classes first, and later, depending on my schedule, we'll determine the best way for me to begin learning her technique.

Very early this morning I called Balanchine and arranged an appointment for him to hear Dickinson's music and give me his opinion. I carried my tape recorder and even though the school is pretty close, the trip took forever. I had to stop and rest my arm two times per block. Balanchine listened and read the score and even though he didn't say that he particularly liked the music, I think he did. At any rate, he told me that it's a work that I should do because of the technical difficulties that the rhythmic and metric irregularities present. He added, "with this, you can do something very beautiful." He gave the class, which was excellent, as always. Violette Verdy and Diana Adams were there and Balanchine put the three of us together to interpret his combinations. Afterwards, I took *adagio* class with Nicholas Magallanes; I lacked confidence because I hadn't been there for two months, but everything turned out pretty well.

I got tickets for the Bolshoi Ballet. Kenneth Dewey got in line at two in the morning and so we were able to get tickets for five performances! We're up in the nosebleed section, but we'll find some way of seeing the performance.

April 14

I'm listening to the music for my new ballet, which I like more each time I hear it. The eight piano pieces contain a great variety of rhythms and harmonies. It's going to take some work to memorize the score but I don't think it's impossible. With the exception of one or two measures, I can now read it. I've selected four dancers: Gloria Govrin, Hester Fitzgerald, Alberta and Alexandra Vernon. The former is one of the apprentices in the company. Her technique, I think, is marvelous, and she's also got style and brains, but the latter one is the best. She's a dancer at the Ballet Russe and is simply divine. Today I asked her if she'd accept and she was thrilled with the offer. The only thing that worries me is that she stands out so much that before long Balanchine might notice her and take her away.

I'm a little sad because I woke up with foot trouble. I couldn't take any more of the barre. Yesterday, I had a rehearsal with the company and even though I'll be dancing *Symphony in C* again, I'm in different movements, so it's like I'm learning a new ballet. Rehearsal went well. I received the review in which Balanchine's company was panned. Even though it hurts, I have to recognize that what the journalist said was true.

I'm going through a crisis. I know that this excess amount of work doesn't leave me any time to think and analyze my actions. The result is that every day I know myself less and I make a lot of mistakes that build up without being corrected. Even though I'm an artist, I somehow find myself leading a complicated, hurried life. I'm planning to thoroughly examine my conscience in order to correct or replace some of my moral principles. I've also realized that I really don't know much about the people around me. In my mind there's a goal and my path has only one lane. I go running ahead all in a hurry, always distracted, thinking about the world of Dostoyevsky, Tolstoy, or Juan Ramón Jiménez. When I go to a meeting, I try to present myself as honestly as possible, but I don't try to see who's hiding behind the faces surrounding me. I've lived in the United States for three years and I can't say that I'm close to classifying the complex mix of bloodlines that make up this nation.

April 19

I just got back from a concert in which Judy Friedman was the soloist. She performed Schumann's *Piano Concerto in A Minor*. She played wonderfully and I got so emotional that I started to cry. Judy looked very handsome in her red satin dress, with her hair loose and her dancer's bearing.

Yesterday I saw *Romeo and Juliet* danced by Galina Ulanova. I don't want to give my opinion of the Bolshoi Ballet because *Romeo and Juliet* can't really be considered a ballet. It's a theatrical production with a great set and costumes in which the dancing plays a secondary role. Ulanova deserves my respect. She dances well and her body seems as young and flexible as a ballerina of thirty. I think that every dancer or person interested in art should see this company, because by seeing it, you learn the history of ballet. The Bolshoi is a magnificent museum piece because it shows what ballet was like during the last century. Thanks to this knowledge, we can begin to see how far ballet has come, from a *Romeo and Juliet* of the Bolshoi to an *Agon* of the New York City Ballet; the whole story lies there. The ballet of our time has done away with the superfluous and has encountered the essence of dance. From a trend toward the baroque and lavishness we have developed a pure line, a dance which stands for the beauty of dance itself in communion with music. It's the same process that has taken place in the other arts and, if you analyze it, it's the fruit of several different sources. The individual who lives and breathes within the atmosphere of the new dance era remains, however, untouched by the choreography of Russian ballet. It is a living museum piece that has wonderful bodies, though it doesn't have contemporary choreographers who are independent and seek new forms of expression and movement.

April 20
My foot is better and I'm studying Dickinson's music. Today Judy Friedman dropped by the house. We finished rehearsing at three-thirty and by four we were studying the score. The work is so absorbing and interesting that at seven-thirty we realized we hadn't eaten anything. I'll begin rehearsals with the dancers next Wednesday.

April 23
At the first rehearsal yesterday everything went well. Peter Dickinson played the piano and Rosemary Dunleavy, Veronika Mlakar, Susan Kenniff, and Joan arrived on time. We rehearsed from seven to ten at night. I completed the first variation and began the second one. Today I worked at home from nine to midnight. I now have the basic ideas for the second variation, so I might be able to finish it in tomorrow's rehearsal. Peter is fascinated by my choreography because I've set the piece completely in sync to his music. I've studied so much that I think I've learned more in the last couple of weeks than from all my piano and violin lessons. Judy Friedman has been wonderful; thanks to her, I've been able to analyze every

phrase, every harmony, every rhythm, etc. Peter says that there isn't a detail of the music that I've left out. To make things even better, I knew the first variation by heart before we began rehearsals. So, everything's going very well.

One other thing: Nancy Lassalle came to see me at the school between classes to tell me that Lincoln Kirstein, director of the New York City Ballet, had recommended me to Ted Shawn, one of the most distinguished figures in dance and director of the Jacob's Pillow dance festival. I'll be choreographing a ballet based on a biblical parable with music from the Twelfth Century and will have 15 dancers to work with. Everything will be paid for. I don't know how much I'll be paid, but I'll find out later. This is an important moment for me. It's the first time that Lincoln Kirstein has asked me to do a piece and recognized me as a professional choreographer. I'll have to wrap myself up in the art, customs, and history of the Twelfth Century.

April 29

I've now mounted four of the eight variations that make up Dickinson's musical work. We rehearse for three hours every third day and on the alternate days I study the music and come up with ideas. The choreography is based on rhythm and it's been a great learning experience for me to analyze, study, and memorize the whole work. My tape recorder has been my best friend. I can now read the music easily. I'm not able to hear the sounds, but I can play all of the rhythms, no matter how difficult they are. There are parts where one bar is in $3/4$ time, the following in $5/4$, and the next in $6\frac{1}{2}/4$. The piece has a great deal of variety in its counterpoints and it is fascinating to transform these sounds into movement.

I'm preoccupied by the ballet I'll be doing for Jacob's Pillow. The costumes for the dancers are nearly authentic but very ugly and impractical for movement. The music is choral, in Latin, and the singers develop the parable of "The Wise and Foolish Virgins." I will have five wise and five foolish virgins, two devils, two vendors, Gabriel and Christ. They want me to tell an entertaining tale through dance. Another thing that worries me is that, according to what I've been told, the stage is very small. I'm trying to teach myself about the Twelfth Century, but it's difficult to concentrate because I'm so interested in the Dickinson piece that I even conduct it in my sleep. I'm proud that I can choreograph four variations in only four rehearsals, considering the difficulty of the music.

I saw the Bolshoi version of *Swan Lake*, which I found long. The dancers are wonderful. Balanchine sent 130 tickets to the company as a gift, so on the fourteenth of May we'll have the Bolshoi in the audience. I'm supposed to dance because *Symphony in C* is closing the program.

May 3

I'm being naughty and instead of getting down to studying, I'm writing. For days I've been dying to, although I should be spending all my time on studies and work. I've finished six parts of the Dickinson work and I'm very happy with the results, particularly with a *pas de trois* and a *pas de deux*. In the latter I created an obstacle for myself: during the entire *adagio* the female dancer's left hand is linked to the male dancer's right hand. It's a handicap that has produced movements that are very harmonious and varied. In the *pas de trois* Veronika Mlakar, Susan Kenniff, and Bill Earl dance and they also make sounds—they do this with their hands and hold, sustain, and slice the air. This is also just an idea, but the results are pretty good. I've had a few problems with the girls in the chorus, which means that the end hasn't been resolved yet. Today I'll work on Bill's variation. It's slow and very difficult to develop with masculine movements.

I've got a lot of books on Romanesque art and I study them from time to time. I'll start rehearsals on the eleventh. I should complete the variations so that my mind can be at ease and I can concentrate on the parable. I'm happy that this is turning out to be my destiny.

May 8

I'm now working on the twelfth-century ballet. Yesterday I held an audition at twelve-thirty in one of the salons of the School of American Ballet. A lot of pretty young girls showed up, most of them between thirteen and fourteen years old and good dancers. It was hard to get rid of some of them when the auditions ended. I set them a combination that I invented for the religious music that Dr. Ethel Thurston had sent me. It was a bit difficult, inspired by the sculpture of the Twelfth Century.

I'm very tired but quite satisfied with the choreography that I created for Dickinson's music. It isn't completely done, I've got two or three minutes to go, but I should put it aside and concentrate on the other.

54

Judy Friedman has come over at night to help me study music and create choreography. At times she acts as my mirror. She corrects my line and the tempo of the movements I compose for the music. For two nights we've worked from eight till twelve-thirty.

The Director of the Jacob's Pillow Festival is Ted Shawn. He's famous for being obviously homosexual and very tight with money. The "salary" they're paying me for my work is laughable: the dancers get $20 per performance, and I get $50, room and board, transportation, a pianist, and costumes. The biggest joke is that I'll probably have to sacrifice the $50 for tunics because the ones they offered me were horrible.

May 9

Today I saw the last of the Bolshoi programs. It's a great company and I'm not sorry I spent as much as I did on it. The Bolshoi has the tradition and power of two centuries of education. Putting aside my opinion about the company's approach to dance, I respect and admire it. Each member is a consummate athlete and a sculpture full of life. I think that their trip to America will benefit us and I hope that it influences them. On Monday we'll dance for them: *Agon*, *Serenade*, and *Symphony in C*. I hope that they can discover the variety of dimensions that exists in dance and understand the depth that can be achieved through dance. I think that Balanchine has planned to teach them something new, but mixed in with ballets that aren't so advanced, because if you subjected them to a real first-rate program, they'd become hysterical and laugh, and wouldn't absorb anything. Balanchine is quite generous to help them get out of the rut they're in, but they are marvelously trained. Their acrobatics, their dances full of character, strength, and joy are delightful.

May 11

On Mothers' Day I had a rehearsal with the New York City Ballet and afterwards I worked on creating ideas for my new ballet. Judy Friedman helped me as usual. I'm very grateful to her because she's taken so much interest in my work and gives me almost all of her free time. Today I'm taking class at ten and at noon I'm dancing for the Bolshoi—it's going to be a rehearsal with orchestra and a Russian audience. Later we'll be going to the mezzanine where we're hosting a buffet so that both companies can get to know each other. It's too bad that because I don't speak Russian, I won't really get to know any of them.

I don't know what's happened with *Huapango* and the Ballet Concierto. I don't want my works to be filed away, and as far as money is concerned, maybe I'm not worried because I don't have any. For the time being, I have enough to eat and I think that it's more important for the ballets to be in someone's repertoire than for me to receive a fistful of paper and coins. So, it's really up to my parents to send me the letter I mentioned and have me sign it. That way the ballet will be remembered before the dancers make a mess of everything and force things to a halt. On the fourteenth I'm dancing for the first time in the new season, which opens tomorrow, Tuesday the twelfth.

May 12

Today was an historic day in which the New York City Ballet and the Bolshoi got to know each other personally. We danced *Agon*, *Symphony in C*, and *Serenade* for them. The orchestra accompanied us, but it wasn't a regular program, only a rehearsal with interruptions, corrections, etc. From Ulanova on down, the entire company was in the house. Afterwards we offered a splendid buffet, but sadly we didn't have any interpreters and with one or two exceptions, none of us could strike up a conversation and get to know any of them.

This company's visit to America is very important; I should write something about it, but I'm afraid of being too frank and then misunderstood. As dancers I think they're wonderful. Their technique is fantastic, even though it's a little sloppy on stage. They don't worry about closing their fifths, or stretching their knees, and they concentrate on expression and acrobatics. The artistic level of the company seems impoverished to me. Their dance is purely superficial and only reaches the point of being "entertaining." Their full ballets turn into galas of decorations, costumes, lights, and so on. But the steps are repetitive and the only thing that is consistent is the beauty of their acrobatics. It's a company that may entertain an audience for a while, but it doesn't move them. Of course, it has its value as an authentic relic, a museum piece that shows us ballet from more than a century ago.

Their stars are marvelous. Ulanova is the ideal. She is something more than a ballerina. She has been idealized by the world and despite her age she keeps dancing; with each of her performances, she is received with the greatest enthusiasm. Maya Plistetskaya is marvelous, she's got everything: personality, beauty, technique, elegance, etc. Timofeyeva, Maximova, Chistova, Kondratieva are all examples of the perfect ballerina. The men are strong, handsome, and seem to fly over the stage. Their character dancers are fantastic. Each one of them is a "Stradivarius." They form a great company; they are terrific acrobats and artists, but this day and age requires something much more from art.

May 14

Yesterday I held a three-hour rehearsal for *The Wise and Foolish Virgins* and regret to say that it did not go well. My ideas were few and far between, and I spent three hours struggling to work something out of the first theme in the ballet. The music is very monotonous, which doesn't help me. I don't think I'm going to be able to create something that looks good and is enjoyable to dance. Oh well, if I achieve the first I'll feel calm. It's too bad that this will be my first ballet for the highly educated dance public. God help me!

Today I'll dance at City Center. I'll do more than I did last year and in two movements I'm fairly stage-forward although in the grand finale I'm the last one in the last line. Today will be the premiere of *Episodes*, a strangely constructed ballet which has two choreographers, one classical and one modern: Martha Graham and George Balanchine. She'll dance the principal part in the modern episode. The music is Webern's, but I don't know what kind of salad they've created because part of it is pure Bach.

May 20

My schedule is full of work. At ten in the morning I'm already at the school and I don't make it back home until five in the afternoon. I take class and rehearse *The Wise and Foolish Virgins*, which is coming along slowly but seems to be taking shape.

At night, I dance in the theater, sometimes. Other times, I attend as a spectator and still others I rehearse the Dickinson from eight to eleven at night. I think this is a good ballet. Peter Dickinson is working on the orchestration of the piece and has already completed three variations. He's doing it in the form of a concerto for piano and orchestra. We have a lot of plans for this ballet. I would like to present it in Mexico next year. Maybe with the help of the British Consul we can arrange for Peter to go to Mexico for the premiere and conduct the orchestra as a guest-artist. I don't know what Balanchine or Martha Graham will say when I show it to them, but in my opinion, it's a good work. It has force, line, and a theme. Well, time will determine the future of this ballet.

June 1

Sunday I went down to see *Gagaku*. It was performed by a group of dancers and musicians from the Imperial House of Japan whom Lincoln Kirstein had brought to New York. They're all men, from very young to fairly mature. Their dressing room is next to ours; it was given to the apprentices last season, with the only difference being that once it was a bare room without lights or make-up tables and now it's a first-rate dressing room, adorned with transparent gauze, satin, brocade, and carpets. Since the artists have always lived in the Imperial House, it would have caused them a bit of a nervous shock to find themselves in a closet.

I hadn't had the opportunity to see *Gagaku*. We'd run across each other in the hallways and I'd had the opportunity to admire the elaborate kimonos and the strange and symbolic musical instruments that they use to develop their dances. They're all extremely courteous and speak a little English, with the help of dictionaries that they always carry. They're quite gallant, too. While I was examining a kind of black wooden lance I exclaimed, "Beautiful!" and he replied, "No, *you* are beautiful." *Gagaku* has the beauty of a religious rite: the players express solemnity, absolute concentration, and perfect control in each movement, and the music is exotic. They can make your stomach sag very low and something tells you that you're seeing the representation of centuries of artistic refinement. Eastern art is so different from Western that for most of the spectators it's boring because "nothing happens." The choreographic developments are very simple and series of movements are continuously repeated. Nonetheless, it has great aesthetic value and its solemnity inspires tremendous respect; it makes me want to hold my breath for fear of interrupting the artist. *Gagaku* is not popular in Japan. It has to do with the court and the "scholars," people who dedicate their lives to study. I wish I could study each of the instruments and know the significance of each of the dances. Maybe I'll be able to and then I'll write an article that might prove interesting.

While I was watching the musicians and the orchestra, a little Japanese man approached me and began to explain what my eyes were watching with such curiosity. One of the musicians submerged his instrument in some kind of white urn, and the voice in my ear said, "he's warming it up." After various explanations, the voice asked, "Are you Gloria?" Surprised, I turned around and answered, "How did you know?" It turns out that this young man had heard about me from one of his friends who lives at International House and knows about my wanderings in New York.

Today I returned to hard work and continued choreographing the ballet of the virgins. I still can't tell if it's good or bad, but I've got half of it done, and as it develops it's becoming more interesting.

June 7

My performances with the New York City Ballet are over, maybe forever. One thing I do know is that I don't want to do *Symphony in C* again. My ballet will be presented in Massachusetts on the twenty-fourth. I hope to present the Dickinson ballet at the end of next week. I'll speak to Balanchine and see what happens. There's a young choreographer named Marvin Gordon who wants to form a company and is interested in my work. I regret not dancing in my own pieces. But, after all, this seems to be my future.

June 11

It's two in the morning and it's not the best hour to write, but New York is very hot and I can't sleep. My apartment isn't air-conditioned. This morning, while I was taking class, I asked myself which was better—a short summer or winter. It seems as if we have a short spring every year, but this year has been different. My home is very close to the Hudson River. I can see the water from my window and its breeze is fairly refreshing. We have all of the windows open to help the air circulate. This makes everything black, but I keep after it and I nearly always have the house presentable. I feel a sense of relaxation and satisfaction from housekeeping. It's something completely different from my career and it keeps me distracted and entertained. André Egelvsky will go to Mexico with a group of dancers from the New York City Ballet, among them, Melissa Hayden, Barbara Walzak, Patricia Wilde, Janice Cohen, Edward Villella, and Judith Green. Of course they'll be dancing traditional works. I hope they're well received.

I spoke with Balanchine and we agreed that next Monday he'll come to see my new ballets, *The Wise and Foolish Virgins* and the Dickinson. The former won't be completely finished. That's too bad, because I have about four minutes of music left to set.

Today we had a three-hour rehearsal. I acted like a general and the result was satisfactory. I put my dancers on a military regimen and only then could I see the patterns and lines that until yesterday I only saw in my imagination. It isn't, nor will it be, a great ballet.

But given the monotony of the music, I think I've done quite a bit. It's a ballet based more on the patterns produced by the bodies than on the personal expression of the soloists. The three male dancers, Freddie Herko, Alan Bergman, and Bill Earl are good and have handsome physiques. I have ten girls. Many of them are beginners, but they all have good technique and line.

I'm happy with the Dickinson piece. Today we rehearsed it for two hours, from eight to ten, and it looks very good. The dancers are first-rate and I think the choreography is pretty good, too. In Judy Friedman's opinion, it's the best thing I've done. It's modern in conception, idea and expression, and very interesting. The music is simply wonderful, even though the first time you hear it, it may sound dissonant and absurdly modern. But if one experiences the music and the dancing together, it's easy to understand.

And speaking of Dickinson, it's very possible that he'll make a trip to Mexico, which would be as nice as receiving $25,000. It's like this: My friend Bob Verberkmoes, the set designer with the idea for *Malinche*, is now working on the set and the libretto for *Malinche*. But we need a good composer to do the music. I wrote to Carlos Chávez, but I didn't even receive a reply. Dickinson has talent and youth, a need to create and faith in my work. But he's English. He will have to get to know my country, its music, its history and with the impression that all of this produces he should be able to write a first-rate work. The German Offenbach wrote the best and most representative French music and Rimsky-Korsakov wrote an Italian score. The only Spanish symphony belongs to Lalo. Why not Dickinson the Mexican? He's arranging for them to cover the costs, but he can only go to Monterrey. I'd like him to be able to go to Mexico City. But in this case he doesn't have the money and, as always, I thought of the possibility of my family giving him room and board. It wouldn't break them and I don't think he'd be a bother. Peter is very clean, pleasant, and decent, and I think that he'd be a good accompanist for my father on the Steinway. He wouldn't stay long and it might help produce a great musical work that I could use to choreograph *Malinche*.

June 13

Today I rehearsed the two ballets and I'm very happy. The poor dancers are dead. Imagine the schedule: class from eleven to twelve-thirty, rehearsal for *The Wise and Foolish Virgins* at four-thirty and then Dickinson from eight to eleven at night.

Yesterday I spoke to Balanchine by phone because three of my girls have final exams next Monday at four in the afternoon, the same time that I'd arranged for him to watch the rehearsal. I convinced him to come on Saturday morning instead. So tomorrow, at three in the afternoon, I'll show him my two latest works.

June 15
Balanchine sees *The Wise and Foolish Virgins* and *Vitálitas*

My people began to fill the studio at three in the afternoon. Everyone was there: all of the girls were pretty, tall, shapely in pink tights and black leotards, the boys handsome in black tights and white shirts. I gave the only touch of color to my soloist, Veronika Mlakar, whom I dressed in black and red. All of their faces showed some anxiety and the atmosphere was so charged it was electric. I was very calm, maybe because I didn't have to dance, even though I knew that what was about to be performed in a few minutes was my creation. Appearing tall and thin in a tailored brown suit, Peter Dickinson looked almost handsome. Dr. Ethel Thurston was dressed simply, her full skirts well-suited to her ample body. Everyone was waiting for the moment when the door would open and Balanchine would walk in. But the minutes passed and Balanchine didn't arrive. To distract them I began to rehearse with Dickinson. We ran through it once completely and it looked so good that everyone was impressed. Knowing Balanchine's usual punctuality, I couldn't wait any longer. So I went into the office, picked up the telephone and called everywhere until I found him. Ten minutes later, he arrived.

At the end of *The Wise and Foolish Virgins*, I approached him and he gave me his opinion. "The ballet is good," he said, "and it's inventive, despite the difficulties that the music presents because of its monotony." The ballet didn't bore him for an instant. He liked it because I used the story of the virgins as secondary material, so the force of the ballet is located in the dance itself and not in the storyline that inspired the dance. Each development captures the attention of the spectator and reveals something new within me. The ballet isn't finished and Balanchine gave me a wonderful idea. I said that the role of Christ bothered me in the sense that it didn't seem appropriate to represent him with the body of a dancer. God is something infinite and it would be profane to try and say "Christ moved in this way, or acted in this way, or was this handsome or this ugly." I no longer feel the need to create a part for him. Balanchine agreed with me and told me to use a light instead of a man. This seemed perfect.

The ballet develops as follows: the virgins dance, and the archangel Gabriel arrives and reveals to them the existence of the light. Each one takes her small lamp and dances. Some of them take care not to run out of oil, while the others forget the value of the flame and lose it while they're sleeping. When they discover what's happened, they run desperately toward their sisters, who only have enough for themselves. The merchants refuse to sell oil to the poor fools and they can no longer light their lamps. (I've completed the choreography up to this point.) Christ arrives. The light begins to shine from a corner, but the moment the foolish virgins try to approach it, the ray disappears and emerges from the opposite corner of the stage. Thus, the foolish virgins chase after the light without ever capturing it. Toward the end, three devils invade the stage, which is now lit in blue and red, and they perform a ballet of contortions and tortures, making the bodies of the foolish virgins appear shapeless before transforming them into a horrible mass. In the background will be a staircase with five steps, on each, a pure virgin; then the five bodies will be bathed in light. The End.

Then we performed *Vitálitas* and God helped me by adding the final touch of a storm that made the lights go out. You could only see the bodies in shadow and the ballet's power was magnified by the elements. When the work ended, Balanchine looked me straight in the eye and didn't hide his sentiments. He told me the ballet was good, very good. We spoke for a long time, or to be more precise, Balanchine spoke to Thurston, Dickinson, and me. He spoke about the choreography he'd just seen, about the details that he liked best, about me and my talent. I didn't know what to say because it's very embarrassing to hear praises fall from such respected lips, and in front of strangers. During his conversation he told me to guard against my enemy: the desire for fame and money. He recommended work and modesty. He's a great genius and I wished that I could have recorded his words. There's no real danger. I know that it takes a lifetime to become a good choreographer and I've decided to devote mine to achieving this.

Balanchine spoke about the state of dance around the world. He said he doesn't like any of it—in France, England, Russia, etc.—because, according to him, none of the choreographers understand that dance is dance. They want to turn it into the bastard brother of the other arts. They can't accept dance that doesn't describe something. He compared it to flowers: a garden is beautiful because of its form, its color, not because one flower falls in love with another, or because one of them killed the other at its side. What is Mozart? Music. Simply music. It's not necessary to give a name to a symphony—you don't have to call it *The Clock* or *The Waterfall*. It's the same with dance. Balanchine said that I could create because I understood this and because I could dance well and because I knew which images I wanted to develop. He spoke about Jerome Robbins as a genius, one of the few geniuses of choreography, and he made me realize that despite the fact that he's very famous today, he worked years to achieve his fame. He told me "we must defend our art from superficiality and degeneration. There's nothing worse than a bad ballet. People are being diplomatic when they say they don't go to the ballet because they don't understand it. No, they're simply bored by it, because movement without value only hypnotizes them and puts them to sleep."

He's going to dedicate the coming year to Latin America and he urged me to work with Chávez, Revueltas or any other composer who interested me. I spoke to him about my letter to Chávez and his complete silence. "After all, he's Minister of Education," he said with irony, "but I'll write him and I'll tell him that you're my student and we need his music." He congratulated me on the results I'd achieved with my dancers and said that it was wonderful for them. My group looked better than many companies throughout the world and I was very gratified by how well they danced. This is history. I'm very grateful that Balanchine didn't allow me to enter his company. Had this happened, at the end of this season all I would have had was a tired body and a tired soul. Instead, I've produced two works that have value. "Are you going to give them to the Mexicans?" he asked me. "If they ask me, I will," I replied.

June 18

My choreographic production owes much to the continuous current of emotion that is sent to me from my home. Art has no value in and of itself. My work is for others. I fight to improve and to offer something satisfactory. Last night, Wayne Richardson, a highly cultivated man, a theater director and authority on Greek tragedy, came to the rehearsal of Dickinson's work and his reaction was very favorable. What impressed him the most was the Mexican flavor that one feels throughout the ballet! "It's like *Huapango*." I never wanted to do a work in the Mexican style. I simply began to develop figures and movements to the rhythm of the work, and my only goal was to create emotion through movement. Nevertheless, *Huapango* is very Mexican. Wayne thinks the same thing about my Dickinson ballet. It's purely classical, but the force of the environment I grew up in and which I'm still so connected to emerges in my creations. I hope to be able to present the Dickinson to the Mexicans. I know that Balanchine was very impressed with the work and I sincerely believe it's good enough for the New York City Ballet. But the fight is hard and the obstacles to getting recognized are innumerable. I know that sooner or later it will happen, but for the time being I want my ballets to be in circulation. A ballet in the archives is a dead ballet. The only stage I have at present is Bellas Artes. Mexico should get to know my work.

Today I got through the part of Christ for *The Wise and Foolish Virgins* and I finished half of the devil's part. So tomorrow, or Friday at the latest, I'll have the work ready. Next Tuesday we'll be at Jacob's Pillow. We'll run lights and check costumes for the performance on the twenty-fifth. I've had a few discussions with Nancy Lassalle. She's against the idea of using a light as a symbol of Christ. She gives me a thousand arguments against it, she calls me unfeeling, she thinks I'm carrying two distinct interpretations in the same ballet, etc. But frankly, I think I'm right. What is God? I don't know and nobody else knows. How can you give Him human form? How can you make a single gesture speak for the enormity of the absolute? I will use the light.

June 27
Trip to Jacob's Pillow
After traveling 700 miles in three days, I'm now in Southampton. Last Tuesday Graciela de Majo, Kenneth Dewey, Lou and I left for Massachusetts in our little car. Kenneth, a playwright who has studied theater and knows about lights and stage direction, was in charge of the lighting for *The Wise and Foolish Virgins*. The dancers went by bus and left New York at eight-thirty in the morning.

The theater at Jacob's Pillow was a pleasant surprise. It's large and rustic. It's in a lovely setting reminiscent of La Marquesa or the Desierto de los Leones near Mexico City. Much to our surprise, the weather was fairly cool and we found ourselves inappropriately dressed. Nancy Lassalle arranged for Lou and me to stay in Lenox, a nearby town with a first-rate hotel. For various reasons, we arrived three hours late. The rehearsal was at four in the afternoon. The choreography had been perfectly rehearsed and the dimensions of the stage were ideal so we didn't have to worry about the dancing.

The lights, on the other hand, were a huge problem. Ken had to put up with the group of long-faced, rude, "experimental" stagehands who were in charge. The rehearsal lasted two hours, and at the end of it the stagehands left without achieving any of the necessary effects.

Ted Shawn, owner of the theater, is an old man of 75 years or so. He's famous for his parties and as the teacher of Martha Graham and other significant figures in modern dance. He's a direct descendent of Isadora Duncan's style and now he doesn't even like modern dance, or classical for that matter. He's only interested in ethnic and religious dance.

After watching the rehearsal, we had a chat. Ted Shawn hadn't expected a classical ballet. His idea was to present a piece that was a religious service, but on stage. What bothered him the most was that it was danced on point: he said that in the Twelfth Century, ballet didn't exist and how could I dare do something from that epoch on point? Could the girls dance on half-point? The audience was mainly going to be Christians who were interested in introducing the dance into religious services. The purpose of presenting the dance in the festival, he said, was to give those prelates an idea of the kind of representations that could be performed. He said my work was too theatrical and would be out of place. I replied that this was the first time I ever heard that idea, that I'd been called upon to create my version of a biblical parable set to music of the Twelfth Century. Never for a moment had it been my intention to reproduce a work from that era—something that would not only be absurd but also impossible because there isn't even a written description of the movements used in the dances of that period. In fact, the only thing that remained was Romanesque art, mostly in French cathedrals, and I'd studied its sculpture and painting as a basis for a twentieth-century ballet. As far as dancing on point or half-point, I replied, my choreography couldn't and wouldn't be altered. Even if it were danced on half-point, it would be impossible for his little "priests" because, I explained, it wasn't the point that made the ballet, but a technique that only professional dancers can acquire after long years of study. I created a ballet for point. The dancers' long, thin lines suggest the sculptures of the Twelfth Century; they're similar to El Greco for that reason.

Then we went to New Boston where a succulent meal had been prepared for us, in a lovely restaurant set amid giant trees. Since there were nineteen in my company and five or six others, we took up the entire dining room. We ate happily but my people made so much noise that Nancy kept giving me troubled looks, which I ignored and didn't pass along to my girls, letting them laugh as they would. The next day we went to a beautiful place, a lake formed from man-made marble quarries. There are probably several springs there, because the lake is green, clear and very deep. It was wonderful to be able to walk in the woods, breathe the fresh air and rest my ears from the noise that accosts one in the city.

The performance began at eight-thirty and I wasn't able to see the numbers that preceded mine because I was helping my dancers get ready. A few minutes before my ballet was presented, I ran to the auditorium. The ballet was great and my dancers were wonderful. The group looked very professional, even better than some famous companies. Each of the dancers had line, technique, and youth. I didn't like the costumes very much, but they weren't awful. Among the standouts were Rebecca McGriff, Susan Kennif, and Rosemary Dunleavy. But everyone did very well and I was happy to have gathered such an excellent group, which also included Dorothy Buck, Helen Heineman, Ruthann King, Claire Mesnard, Alice Glen, Joysanne Sidimus, Barbara Sandonato, William Earl, Alan Bergman and Fred Herko. Joysanne had worked with me in *El mercado* before Judy replaced her.

Concerning my work, I'll say that it's a well-constructed ballet, with a lot of invention and great variety. It's entertaining and appealing, but it's a light piece. It doesn't really produce an emotional impact on the audience. I was pleased with it, and I think that resolving all of the problems that this ballet presented taught me a lot. The audience liked it very much, but because it was a religious ceremony, applause was prohibited. Nevertheless, some people just couldn't help themselves. Ted Shawn didn't even say thank you, and I didn't send him my regards.

Each of the dancers received a box with nougat and a card with my thanks. They gave me a beautiful bouquet of roses and carnations and a sweet card. From there we went to a restaurant where we spent most of the night dancing mambos, rumbas, rock and roll, and so on. I was happy and I think that for my girls it was an unforgettable evening. Lou and I spent seventy-five dollars.

The funny thing about this is that I had to cover the technical and transportation costs and didn't get a cent for all my work. They offered me fifty dollars, but I turned it down. Maybe it was absurd of me, but that amount seemed offensive: I'd rather be magnanimous and present my work for free than accept meager payment. The dancers received twenty dollars, tights, point shoes, transportation, lodging and food. Nancy helped cover expenses.

July 9

Regarding Jacob's Pillow, I received a check for fifty dollars in the mail, and even though I'd sworn not to accept it, I've decided to cash it. Nancy Lassalle spoke with me yesterday and, in a manner of speaking, offered apologies for the incidents at Jacob's Pillow.

I took class with the company. It was good and hard, and it was nice to see all the boys and girls again. Even though I'm not a member of the company, I feel like a part of it. Yesterday I went to the Ballet Theatre to take class and I found Balanchine's picture among the hundred or so photographs of dancers and choreographers who have belonged to the Ballet Theatre. When I saw it, I smiled and, in my imagination, blew him a kiss.

I'm trying to put together a group of young choreographers who will work together to move the dance world of our generation a step forward. Balanchine is a genius, but life must go on. Sadly, a day will arrive when he will no longer be able to create, and if a young force isn't in place to take the weight off his shoulders, then dance will be condemned to becoming fossilized again. I've spoken with Wayne Richardson and he agreed to act as the group's director. The other choreographers I have in mind, aside from myself, are Paul Taylor (under Martha Graham), Francisco Monción (Balanchine), and Bill Sandberg (from Sweden). We'd only meet when we were presenting our choreography, but as far as creating our pieces, we'd act separately to avoid friction, intrigue, and destructiveness. I already have my group and in a few months my repertoire will be large and varied enough to put on my own performances. I do think, however, that a union composed of various creative artists would strengthen the group and give us more of a voice.

I've discovered a training workshop for the body. It's a rehabilitation service established by a German Jewish woman named Carola Trier. It's fascinating: fat women can become slim and those who are thin can become real beauties. Carola makes use of diverse sets of apparatuses to develop strength, flexibility, and control of the muscles. She has an extremely perceptive eye and as soon as she saw me she recognized my weak points, such as the metatarsal in my left foot that has lost its strength because of my accident at the Fábregas. There are other things that need correction so I'm happy to have discovered this repair shop. Carola will not only improve my line, but also my technique.

July 18

It's the weekend and I'm in Southampton. Last week was so tough that I'm finding it hard to walk. I hadn't danced for three weeks because of my choreography and now I'm trying to return to training. Balanchine gave classes last week, and on top of that I worked with Carola Trier and in the rehearsals. Yesterday, when I came home from work, I filled the tub and dived into the hot water. After that I gave my muscles a good rubdown with Ben Gay and took a nap.

Huapango and *El mercado* are going well. In three rehearsals we've made a lot of headway and the dancers are showing great enthusiasm. I haven't spoken about them: Rosemary Dunleavy is very thin and on the plain side. She's a dancer with amazingly strong technique. She can do anything, no matter how difficult. Her temperament is cold, however, and her dancing is inexpressive. I am working to make her change a few things and if she does what I ask of her, we might achieve something. I gave her Anita Cardús's role in *Huapango*.

Veronika Mlakar will dance Cora Flores's part, but since she's going to be in France for a few months, I'm also teaching it to Rebecca McGriff. Rebecca has a Mongolian type of beauty. Her eyes are large and blue and her cheekbones are very prominent. She's technically strong and graceful and has the ability to dance in phrases that knit together many movements. Her arm-gestures are smooth and elegant and she has a lot of expressive force. In *The Wise and Foolish Virgins*, she was the best dancer and for that reason I thought she'd be wonderful in *Huapango*. It's strange and I don't know why, but she's the least effective dancer in the latter piece. She executes all the steps perfectly well but she turns them into something else. She makes them gentler, sweeter and translates them into a romantic language.

Susan Keniff is the prettiest. She's 16 years old and a model. Her physical beauty is comparable to her expressive force and talent as an actress. She's tall and well formed. Her only failing is that she isn't strong technically. She does everything beautifully on half-point, but as soon as she has to put on her full-point shoes she gets nervous, makes mistakes, and destroys the figures. I'm willing to keep on encouraging her because I know that she can be made into a good artist. She'll play my part as the little sparrow hawk.

Alan Bergman is short with a giant leap, but he's lazy. He has talent, but he doesn't use it. His attitude about dance reminds me of young men who like baseball. Nevertheless, he has style and under my direction he's working well. I won't mention the rest of them, but all in all I have eight dancers for these two ballets. All of them have to learn all the parts, which will help them develop as theatrical dancers.

Regarding the ballet I'll do for the New York City Ballet—if that becomes a reality—I've changed my mind. I think it would be a big mistake to use the history of Malinche because the audience would be more interested in the presentation of her personality than in my own dance. I think that I ought to use ballet in its purest form and using nationalism would be a mistake. It will be as Mexican as *Huapango* is, but it won't depend on any legends or literary ideas. I'm trying to get the score before Balanchine leaves so I can study the music while he's away and begin working on it when he returns.

Carola Trier loved my blouses and it occurred to me to ask my parents to get me one or two more, really fine ones, hand-embroidered in the Mexican style. She's a charming person and treats me as if I were paying her (she has refused to take any money from me). She sees me three times a week and this would normally cost fifteen dollars, but when all is said and done, it will be a fair exchange. I think that at my first opportunity I should send her some gifts. Maybe I'll give her the tablecloth I brought from Mexico for Balanchine. It's very beautiful.

August 1

My new dancers are very good to me. The girls are charming and very eager to get to work. Today we had the rehearsal for *Huapango* and *El mercado*. I taught them Margarita Contreras's variation first and they liked it a lot. We worked from three to six in the afternoon.

August 17

Today I spoke with Balanchine and we're seeing each other tomorrow morning. My group has been talking continuously and is dying to get to work. Balanchine told me that he'd spoken with Carlos Chávez, who has several ideas to discuss with me.

All of the schools are closed and I had to rent a room to work by myself. The heat is overwhelming, and because of this weather, I don't do anything but sigh for Mexico and berate myself for returning here. Today I've become a housekeeper. The first thing I did yesterday was to scrub the tub with soap and a brush. Today I'm washing the curtains and doors and polishing the silver.

August 22

I'm in Southampton. Yesterday I took class from nine to ten and from ten to eleven in the morning, then from eleven to one-thirty we finished *Huapango*. I arranged for a gymnasium session in a school connected with Hunter College. It's huge and it has a wonderful floor, dressing rooms, and showers. Dr. Ethel Thurston got it for me. She's the professor who adapted the music for the *Virgins* and who's working on a ballet called *María Magdalena*.

August 30

We just got back from the movies. We went to see a film with Audrey Hepburn called *The Nun's Story*. It made me remember my perfectionist period in high school, when every day I'd write down all my faults and wrestle for spiritual improvement. I think I gained a lot of self-discipline by doing this. During that time I wrote an "S" on my palm to keep myself from talking; later on I ordered a ring with that letter on it for the same purpose. Now I've changed quite a bit and have become used to my faults. I think I should go back to keeping my little book of faults. If you compare the life of a nun to that of a dancer, there are a lot of similarities, but the big difference is that one of them destroys the self and the other develops vanity and pride. Both of them have their masochistic tendencies, but no one could force me to separate myself from my loved ones; on the contrary, it's the intimate contact with them that stimulates me and forms the foundation of my life. We only see each other for short periods of time, but we have never stopped thinking together, remembering the moments lived in the past. I think it's a terrible thing when a young lady becomes a nun basically to destroy her self-esteem and pride, in other words, her self.

September 1

Alvin Ailey is a black choreographer I'm considering for the young choreographers' group. Lincoln Kirstein recommended him highly. Tomorrow he's coming to see my rehearsal and to get to know the other dancers. *Huapango* is coming along very well. I've kept the variation I choreographed for Margarita Contreras as a permanent part of the work. The score by Schoenberg is the most difficult thing I've ever heard. It's going to take me a long time to analyze it.

September 3

The project is on track; yesterday I met Alvin Ailey. He's a strong young man from the same generation as Xavier Francis and the director and choreographer of a small company that has given public performances. I think he liked my ballets and he seems interested in helping me organize what might become a dance company. He'll begin doing a ballet for the audition we have with Lincoln Kirstein on October 7th. Wayne Richardson, the director of the group, wants me to do a new ballet for the occasion. Kirstein doesn't know my work although he speaks about it as if he did because of what Balanchine has told him. Anyway, I don't see any pressing need to create another ballet before I set one for the New York City Ballet. I'll try to please him in order to please myself, but I don't want to rush, so I'll see if I can have *Huapango* and *Vitálitas* ready for the seventh.

September 8

I worked for five hours on Friday. I changed several parts of *El mercado* and a little of *Huapango*. Now that they've got some age on them I'm discovering a lot of faults.

I went to class and did fairly well. I'm very happy because my work is opening doors and every day I feel more secure about my future. My work is well-known in artistic circles and has a lot of fans. I love the people who work with me and we've been able to form an environment that's both artistic and harmonious.

I've listened a number of times to Revueltas's *Ocho por radio* and like it quite a bit. In my opinion, it's a "drunken" work by a great artist. It sounds like I'm not fully appreciating the work, but on close analysis it seems to be little more than a portrait of everything typical, and in a certain sense popular, in Mexico. Revueltas's piece suggests a poorly-tuned radio in which eight different stations mix and are heard at the same time. It has eight rhythms and eight tones that compete with each other and struggle to gain the upper hand. My idea is to convert the aural concept into a visual sketch in which eight small groups, each in a different color, represent diverse rhythms and tones, fighting, elbowing each other and trying to become the stars of the show. In the middle of this I'm setting a wake. At this point, a man and a woman carry an imaginary bier full of shadows and pain on stage and are soon interrupted by the rude, deafening rhythms. I think that the steps will have to be similar to those used in folk dancing because of the music's descriptive style. I also think that it would be difficult to turn this piece into something more strictly balletic; it will be more like *El mercado*. It's very short, it lasts five minutes, and in fact I think I should do another piece for the same night. I need the score. I've discovered that Balanchine takes quite a while to realize his ideas. He says he has the orchestral score, and I must have it arranged for piano to allow me to construct the choreography. He promised to bring me the score on Friday and it's Saturday and I still don't have it. In Mexico I know there are paperback versions of Revueltas's works; I'll ask my parents to ask Luis Sandi. I'll commission a good musician to do the adaptation for solo piano. This is very important to me because I want to do the choreography with my own group first; then, when I work with members of the New York City Ballet, I won't have to create under the watchful and critical eye of people who don't know me as a choreographer and only see me as a little girl who takes classes but can't dance as well as they can.

Balanchine called me into his office yesterday. He'd observed the class and he asked me to work alone for half-an-hour every day to improve my feet. He says that they're very strong but not very pretty and that I have to be better than the rest of the people in the company.

September 14
Today I got the score for *Ocho por radio* from the New York Music Library. I felt so happy that I must have looked like a little kid with a new toy. It's the work with the eight instrumental parts: clarinet, contrabass, trumpet, percussion (cymbals, maracas, tambourine), first violin, second violin, cello, and bassoon. The score also has a notebook for the conductor. It must be fantastic to be a conductor. I regret not thinking about looking for the score in the library eight days ago. Now that I know which ballet I'm going to do and have the music, I just discovered that my old friend, the tape recorder, isn't working. Well, we'll fix that.

September 21
I've begun *Ocho por radio*. We worked for three hours today and finished 25 measures. I asked Dr. Thurston to take care of the arrangement and she worked over the weekend. Last night she gave me three pages with the bad news that she doesn't want to continue because it's more difficult than she thought it would be and she

doesn't have the time. So I began the work without having more than the first 55 measures.

This morning I ran into Balanchine on the street and told him about what had happened. He told me that he'd do the arrangement for piano. I also spoke with Edward Bigelow, the gentleman who manages business for City Center, to see if he can get me another pianist. I have ten dancers divided into groups: eight women and two men. The steps are still embryonic and the evolutions don't exist yet, but the most important thing is for me to develop ideas and familiarize myself with the music until it's integrated into my own thoughts and feelings. The weekend was very enjoyable. Jorge, Susy, Barbara, Graciela, Lou and I spent it in Southampton.

September 24
I'm dead tired. Today I had class with Balanchine, after that point class, a rehearsal of the Revueltas, and my music studies. Right now Jorge Ruiz is heating some water for my feet, which I soak in salt water. Balanchine's class is really hard because it's more than a class, it's a revision of each and every one of a dancer's imperfections; something that only the rarest of us can achieve. We spent an hour-and-a-half at the barre and I had an especially unforgettable experience because of the way my body is put together. It's nearly impossible for me to close my tendus to the mark and Balanchine said to me "How is it that you, being a choreographer, can't do it perfectly? The only way that you can correct others is knowing the details of the dance in your mind *and* in your body."

The Revueltas ballet is really amusing. I've got 50 measures done and we're so enthusiastic about it that time just flies. It's fantastically polyrhythmic; it holds six to eight different accents at the same time. I'm amazed by what he can achieve in the keys of G and B minor. Revueltas creates an astounding piece from these keys. The ballet is very arbitrary in its movements and has more character than the fifth position. I have three couples and three girls. Some represent the wind instruments, others the strings, and they push and shove to carry the singing voice. In some cases the movements are based on the strongest rhythmic voice, but there are times when I ignore the trumpet, no matter how loud it shouts, and move my people to the contrabass. All in all, I don't know if it will come out good or bad; all I know is that it's interesting and fun to work on.

I got a letter from Peter Dickinson and he told me that he's completed the orchestration for our ballet. It's a good ballet and I haven't lost hope of seeing it performed by the New York City Ballet. Even though I continue my training, I'm not the one who will be dancing. I like my girls a lot, I direct them, educate them, and correct them, but I can't be part of them. I'm the one who directs and creates and they're the ones who dance.

September 29

A dancer's life is difficult and if it weren't for its strange fascination, only a crazy person would pursue it. I've spent hours at home trying to rest my muscles. After Balanchine, Carola Trier and Revueltas, I almost can't move. Balanchine is giving lessons on Tuesdays and Thursdays and I'm obliged to take them. They're for company members only, which makes me suspect that I'm considered a member. I belong to a fairly rare category. I don't have a contract, I don't receive a salary and I don't dance on stage. But it's true that I work as hard as anyone in the company and I train as if I were Melissa Hayden. I rehearse just like any other dancer and I direct, create and study at the same time. Regarding Carola Trier, through exercise we are trying to stretch my muscles and make them leaner, the same with my knees. It feels like a battering ram every day for long periods, but maybe we'll achieve our goal.

Revueltas fascinates me more every day. His short work *Ocho por radio* is a box of secrets. The first time you hear the music, it doesn't seem of any great value or content, but the more you get to know it, the more you discover its strengths: it plays on rhythms, melodies, has several motifs and all in all is a wonderful piece. God help me create dance that's of the same quality as the music.

October 2

They say that every child carries his own cake. In my case, each ballet carries something with it, with the difference being that it's not money but swollen glands. Since yesterday I've been down in the dumps and feeling like a martyr. It was time for my class with Balanchine and I don't think I've ever had such a long class nor have I ever danced more poorly. Alongside Diana Adams, Allegra Kent, Melissa Hayden, and Violette Verdy, I felt like the ugly duckling. That night Judy Friedman and Suki Shoerer, a new girl in the company, came by to visit. I felt much better in their company. Judy is simply enchanting. They came to help me with the music, but in reality all we did was talk.

Today's rehearsal went fairly well considering that I have a new pianist and a new dancer. My voice is so faint that people can't hear me and this makes it difficult to run the rehearsal. Judy and Hester Fitzgerald, the understudies, are both with the New York City Ballet. Up until now it's been a continual fight between rhythms of a common and noisy nature. Suddenly, with just a few sounds, Revueltas transports us into a sad scene represented by a very simple melody. In my imagination, a funeral wake grows out of this, but I can't resolve it so literally. During the transitional measures five of the six women disappear, leaving only the soloist with three other male dancers. With a gesture, she rids herself of the maracas and then the light fades, leaving only the area with the four dancers illuminated. With classical movements, I transport them to the sad theme (that's the part that I began to create during today's rehearsal). Two of the dancers disappear and the soloist is left alone on stage with her partner. They look at each other and raise their arms as if they were carrying a small bier. I want this idea to be dominant and for the couple to dance an *adagio* without ever quite reaching each other because death is between them. It's very difficult and I'm not satisfied with what I created today. I hope that with some work I can achieve this idea.

Nancy Lassalle just spoke to me. She watched the ballet for a few minutes and had some criticisms. Right now I'm so deeply involved with the ballet that it's impossible for me to see it. I want to get it over with, let it rest, and come back and analyze it later. That's the only way I can be impartial. My group is getting better. With each rehearsal, the dancers are more flexible and more expressive.

October 8

As far as my health, I'm coming out of a bad phase. I eat well, although no fattening foods: protein, fruit, vegetables, juice, milk, etc. In the mornings, I have something quick and filling—orange juice mixed with eggs and an envelope of unflavored Knox gelatin. That way, I have a complete breakfast.

Today I took two classes: one given by Madame Doubrovska and the other by Balanchine. In the second, the competition is incredible. I think that the best dancers in the world, technically speaking, are gathered in that salon. I need a lot of courage to overcome my shyness and complexes. Despite the fact that I'm not tall or slim or striking in appearance, I can dance with a smile on my face.

I care about Balanchine very much and beg God never to be a disappointment to him. He's a man who believes in the infinite possibilities of the human body and who demands perfection based on work. Balanchine always speaks in a well-modulated voice, his temperament is sweet, and he has a searching gaze. His power over the company's dancers is immense, but you see no signs of tyranny in him. He's a benevolent dictator, so to speak, a boss who dominates because he instills respect for his genius in those around him.

The Revueltas ballet is progressing and all I have left to choreograph is 30 measures. I'm happy, even though the ballet doesn't look like I imagined it would. The style is very difficult for the classical dancers and they're suffering a lot.

I've found the score for Revueltas. I'd hidden it so carefully that I couldn't find it. It's almost certain that I'll do another ballet, in addition to Revueltas, for the company. Nancy told me last night that it would have to be a lot longer than *Ocho por radio*. I don't know whose music I'll be setting it to. My group will be dancing *Huapango* at City Center on the 28th of this month, at three in the afternoon, in a private audition for Lincoln Kirstein. This will be the first performance that our group of choreographers will present. Alvin Ailey, Paul Taylor, and I will present our works. I wanted to show the Revueltas too, but Nancy is against the idea. I think it would be better to present it for criticism before showing it to a large audience. Balanchine will see it as soon as it's done, but Kirstein should see it too.

October 9

Revueltas's *Ocho por radio* is simply wonderful. All it requires is listening to it as contemporary music that reflects our age of machines, wars, and the atom. It's a composition that brings to mind the automobile, not horse-drawn carriages. It won't sit well with the man who has an eighteenth-century view of the world. Revueltas is a great musician. You have to study the music as if you were going to conduct it. You have to know which rhythms are carried by the clarinet and which by the contrabass and the trumpet. You've got to cue the violins to enter, feel the maracas and hear the cello and contrabass. It's fantastic. At first, everything seems like a mistake. It doesn't hang together or fall apart; it's impossible for you to count the different measures by putting the accents in the places where you'd least expect them. But as you study it, everything becomes clear and beautiful, assuring you that in this way, and only in this way, could the score have been written.

It's a real adventure for me to choreograph. When I'm studying the score, I become very fearful. You get to learn all of these sounds, they become familiar to you, until you can feel them in your bones, but they're empty in space, they're pale and insipid. What is it that they suggest in space? What forms will occupy the voids created by the sounds? You don't know, just like you won't know if you're creating something of the same quality as that of your companion, the composer. True, after the first rehearsal, this tension relieves itself to give way to many others, but at least the first figures are traced and your imagination has begun to turn the sounds into forms. This period lasts for as long as the musical work does and throughout it a nervous energy pushes you to work at all hours. It's nearly impossible to sleep at night because the rhythms assault you and you try to respond to the questions that the previous day's rehearsal left you with. During the creative stage, you'll surprise yourself frequently and you'll come up with ideas that you never imagined belonged to you. That's how you choreograph, and it's fascinating.

October 13

A tough day for me. I took class with Carola Trier, later with Vladimiroff, then with Balanchine for two and a half hours, and finally with Madame Doubrovska. My legs hurt, but I'm not totally exhausted. As a dancer, you get stronger each day and your body learns to work for many, many hours.

I spoke with Balanchine and it looks certain that I'll do another piece for the company. I still don't know which composer I'll be working with. Yesterday we had a rehearsal of the Revueltas and for the first time I got stuck. I only have a couple of seconds to complete the work and that's where I got tangled up. I worked so hard that I gave myself a headache, but I didn't get anywhere so I took a nap but it was impossible for me to get this problem out of my mind. I turned it around and around, trying to find the solution, until I decided to stop and write.

Tomorrow I've got a rehearsal and I beg God to inspire me. The endings are always difficult. The ballet should end in a climax that leaves the spectator with the strongest possible impression. Finding the closing for a ballet is just as difficult as for a work of literature, maybe so. I hope everything goes well, that Balanchine likes the Revueltas, that the other ballet works out successfully and that my adored family can accompany me during the performances. I don't know when the Pan-American Night will be, probably at the end of December or the beginning of January. I want to revive *Vitálitas* to show it to Lincoln Kirstein the same day I show him *Huapango*. Paul Taylor showed me his ballet. It's totally modern, without shoes, and has some lovely plastic moments, but in my opinion it isn't complete because Paul uses the music as background, not as an integral element. Paul Taylor and Alvin Ailey are the other choreographers who will be showing their works to Lincoln Kirstein.

October 15

I finished the Revueltas yesterday and it wasn't that difficult. I think I found a good ending for it.

Since the Dickinson, that is, *Vitálitas*, Nancy Lassalle has covered the costs of the pianist, studio, costumes, leotards, and shoes for *The Wise and Foolish Virgins*. I've realized that she's an optimistic young woman whose ambition is to become a Lincoln Kirstein.

The ballet that I'm planning will be danced during the same performance as the Revueltas premiere. That program is dedicated to Latin America. Balanchine is doing a work to Chávez's *5th Symphony* and I don't know what else. Francisco Monción will use Villa-Lobos; I'll do two ballets. One will be the Revueltas and the other is *Serenata concertante*, opus 40, by Juan Orrego-Salas, who was born in Santiago, Chile, in 1919. It's an abstract symphony that has no folkloric intentions, but in the composer's opinion it contains the spirit of Latin America. I still don't know what I'm getting involved in, but I'm excited about creating a ballet using symphonic music for the first time.

Like every Thursday, I had three classes today, one after the other and all of them in point shoes. At the end of the last class, it seemed as if someone had smeared chilis over the bottoms of my feet. Balanchine's class is very original. He teaches through conversation and he uses the most unexpected metaphors. He has an active mind and finely developed critical sensibilities. He compares a bad position in an arabesque—i.e. when the foot is crooked, to suggest the idea of a turnout, a difference easily noticed up close—to an American car model that becomes more ostentatious every year but isn't aerodynamically designed and is rarely, if ever, as fast as a European car. It's also common in his class for him to sit down at the piano and improvise a special rhythm to teach the movement he wants (we don't have pianists in his class). Even though I'm not a world-class dancer, I've got enough guts to stand up in front and try with all my heart.

October 18

The symphony by Orrego-Salas isn't a piece I would have selected. It's simple, romantic, and even dull. I don't know what my final judgment of it will be because I often don't like musical pieces until I become acquainted with their structure. My initial reservations seem quite superficial and don't always account for everything that the composer is trying to express. On Friday, Balanchine came by the school and told me to drop by his house and pick up the record. He has the score, but he didn't give it to me because he's working on the piano arrangement. I was indifferent toward the work the first time I heard it. The second time I listened to it I liked it quite a bit and I envisioned images, patterns and forms. That night, when I listened to it again, it struck me as simply awful. Since then, I haven't been able to make it suggest anything; I can't even pay attention to it. Well, if I can make a good ballet out of the music for *Virgins*, maybe I can make a good one with Orrego-Salas.

Yesterday I had a complicated day, as always. From nine to eleven in the morning we rehearsed the *adagio*, the trio, the solo and the end of *Vitálitas*. It seems that for the performance for Lincoln Kirstein on the 28th, I'm going to have to replace one boy and two girls. Bill, the only one who knows the part, leaves on tour tomorrow and, even though it's stupid, I must confess that there are parts I don't remember. After that we had class and I was so tired that I didn't perform well. From one to four in the afternoon was the last rehearsal of the Revueltas. Monday at one-thirty in the afternoon, Balanchine will come to see it. Good luck.

Today, Sunday, I'm taking class with the company and after that I'll have three hours of rehearsal for *Huapango* and four hours for *Vitálitas*. Veronika Mlakar will take the principal role along with Susan Kenniff and Vincent Warren. The other dancers are Rebecca McGriff, Helen Heinemann, Joan Brady and Rosemary Dunleavy. Charles Neil, a young black man, Susan Kenniff, Rosemary Dunleavy and Barbara Sandonato will dance *Huapango*.

I'm pleased that the Revueltas choreography reflects, in my opinion, the characteristics of the music: it's unruly, strong, poignant, satirical and spirited. But I don't believe that I've created anything better than *Vitálitas*. God willing, I hope to surpass that achievement.

October 20

Balanchine saw the Revueltas yesterday. He arrived while we were rehearsing *Vitálitas*. I was dancing and I kept dancing until the end of the piece. Later, in a fairly impromptu fashion, we performed *Ocho por radio*. He liked it a lot and said it was a very savory piece. He suggested that I work a little more on the *adagio* because he found parts of it unsatisfactory. He thought it a bit static. I agree with him. My idea was that of a procession and in truth there are many places in it where the two figures are almost completely still.

Something really funny happened. While I was conceiving the ballet, I had this great idea, but I didn't use it because I thought that Balanchine would do something similar. Many times I create something beautiful but I throw it away. Balanchine has created more than 80 ballets with constant variations and I guess that he's done everything. When we arrived at the part that I was talking about he asked me, "And why didn't you interweave the bodies?" (i.e., the bodies twist until they form a knot which later unties itself). I told him that no one would give me credit, no matter what form I used to present that idea, and I'd be accused of copying it, even if it was my own. I said that I loved his influence and that it was the reason I was spending my life in New York and not Russia or England, but I also told him that more than anything I had to be myself. He said that I was being absurd and that I should never abandon an idea for fear of criticism. He also said that he hadn't invented anything: "The human body is just one of many forms and an attitude or an arabesque has no owner, everything depends on how it is used . . . In ten years' time your work will be totally different and you'll surprise yourself with the development you've experienced, but now and always, use the elements and leave your stamp on them. If you have to borrow, borrow from your family and I am your family." So, I've entered the great family of the New York City Ballet, which I've admired so much and have become a choreographer for, fulfilling a dream that I never imagined possible.

I'm quite happy and everyone is congratulating me. I invited Balanchine to the performance we're doing for Lincoln Kirstein and he said he'd like to come. I'm going to dance the lead role in *Vitálitas*, that is, the one performed by Veronika Mlakar. It's difficult and requires everything—technique, personality, strength, smoothness, etc. I'm really nervous.

We're still holding daily rehearsals and I can tell that my people are tired. I'm worried about *Huapango*. It no longer satisfies me and there are many parts I'd like to revise. For example, the leaps at the end aren't very imaginative and they won't be performed properly; my people have a lot of trouble capturing the spirit of *Huapango*. They simply don't produce the necessary emotion along with pure movement.

Yesterday, after my people danced the Revueltas, I gave each one of them a musical instrument. My group dances very well. I like them and feel grateful to them. My pianist, Gordon Boelzner, is very handsome and young, with marvelous fingers. He's a concert soloist with stage fright. He's also nervous about playing for Balanchine. He came a half an hour early and played the whole thing, note for note, very slowly to be sure that he didn't strike a false chord. It's wonderful to have such a unified group. The only thing that worries me is that I'm becoming very demanding and bossy. Authority can get into your bones.

October 23

I'm happy because yesterday and today I rehearsed the variations that Veronika Mlakar danced in *Vitálitas*, which I'll perform for Balanchine and Kirstein. Peter Dickinson has been kind enough to accompany me on the piano. Yesterday we worked from noon to two-thirty and today from twelve-thirty to four in the afternoon. I think that I've improved significantly with only two rehearsals. The two variations are very difficult because they require technique.

October 26

The date we're supposed to dance *Huapango* and *Vitálitas* for Lincoln Kirstein and Balanchine has been changed again; now it looks as if we'll be doing it on Monday, November 9th at three in the afternoon. Today's rehearsal went fairly well. We went through the Revueltas, the Moncayo, and the Dickinson. My role in this last piece wasn't bad, but it didn't come off as well as it did last Friday. I'm still working on the *adagio* in the Revueltas and I modified the end of *Huapango*, removing the leaps that the three female dancers make when they are lifted by the principal. In its place I created a figure with four people.

This afternoon Wayne Richardson met with Balanchine and Betty Cage, manager of the New York City Ballet. Mr. Balanchine told Richardson how much he was looking forward to the upcoming performance and that he was greatly interested in seeing *Huapango*. He mentioned that I told him I'd completely re-choreographed the work. Balanchine said, "I don't think we have to worry about Gloria, she'll make it," to which Wayne replied "Of course." Betty Cage agreed: "She has it . . ." Balanchine confirmed her point of view: "She certainly has it." I'm terrified of letting them down, especially since they have such high hopes for me. It's hard to explain, but when something like this happens, it makes you feel very small. I'm only a dancer with tenacity, willpower, and energy—God help me.

The Separation and What I Learned

I was never accepted as a member of the New York City Ballet, and my relationship with George Balanchine was completely severed. I often wonder what led to this. After I had my second child, Lorena, I had a very difficult time finding a nanny to take care of her and I remained stranded in Mexico for about ten months before being able to return to New York. Maybe Mr. B. thought that I wasn't as committed to ballet as he expected me to be. I was never able to discuss this with him.

In hindsight I think that this separation benefited me and helped me to grow as an artist and choreographer; in many ways, it permitted me to implement the principles that Mr. B. had taught me. To begin with, after I left the School of American Ballet, I no longer had access to rigorously trained dancers, or to good studios, so I had to create in very difficult circumstances. I had to do ballet in gyms, sometimes on floors that were impossible to work on in point. I also had to incorporate dancers of different backgrounds, some even from different professions, such as actors, or dancers who were less proficient than I was accustomed to. All this forced me to think even more than usual and to design movements that broadened my vocabulary.

Music

Mr. B.'s insistence that I study music has influenced me to the present day. In Brazil, where I worked with Arthur Mitchell to help him found a professional ballet company in Rio de Janeiro, I had no access to taped music. Bach's *Concerto in D minor* was choreographed directly to the score. The first time the company heard the music was in the general rehearsal with the orchestra.

I continued to study music with Eduardo Mata, a Mexican conductor and a friend. Together we developed a method of marking the scores that made it easier for me to recognize whether a bar was regular or irregular. Mata also taught me conductors' tricks that have helped me enormously throughout my career.

Through my friendship with composers such as Peter Dickinson, Mario Lavista, Manuel Enríquez, Federico Ibarra, and many others, I diversified my musical interests and made ballets to music by composers not normally represented in ballet—such as Guillaume de Machaut, Anton von Webern, or Edgar Varèse.

Few choreographers understand music. Both in the classical and modern fields I have observed that music is used as a background curtain, not as an integral part of the ballet. I see again and again the use of external, non-dance elements to justify a lack of choreographic ideas. I agree with Mr. B. that in ballet the most important thing is movement, that movement comes from music and that what isn't conveyed through movement is not important. Once I have fully completed the analysis of a musical score, I begin to choreograph by letting my body freely improvise to the music. Ideas are generated through movement.

During my career I have remained an abstract choreographer. On rare occasions I have created ballets with a narrative structure, but even in these cases the creative process remains the same. The secret is to master the music and storyline so deeply that it becomes second nature and you can forget about them when you begin to create.

Handicaps
Concerning handicaps or problems to be resolved, which Mr. B. advised me to incorporate into my pieces, I've tried all kinds of different possibilities to the extent that any time I feel comfortable with something, I change it. Among the handicaps I've established for myself are: building a visual equivalent to a fugue, choreograph-ing to the rhythm of poetry, creating a *pas de deux* in which the dancers never let go of each other's hands, or starting and ending a dance with the same body sculpture. Mr. B. liked to take a phrase and change and elaborate it in many ways. I've done that in some of my pieces, but through the years I've found that sometimes it's best to trust intuition and not to re-elaborate ideas too much. This approach was possibly my first divergence from Mr. B.'s principles.

The Human Figure
I remained faithful to the idea that the choreographer must broaden her study of the arts in general—music as well as visual and other arts. Sometimes it led me to very different conclusions from those of Mr. B. In the '70s and '80s, I traveled extensively through Europe and came in direct contact with works that I'd already seen in New York, but now they made a stronger impact on me. Specifically, the works of Rodin helped me transform my perception of ideal beauty.

Looking at Rodin's sculptures encouraged me to pursue an ideal that was less dance-oriented. At that time, the standards of beauty in ballet were terribly limited to the pursuit of an extremely thin figure. I didn't want my dancers to look only like those idealized in classical ballet. I wanted my dancers to look like Rodins or Michelangelos; I wanted them to look closer to life. My contact with art helped me re-encounter the human figure. I've also wanted to fully incorporate the sexual dimension of the human body as an important part of artistic expression.

The Dancer

I've danced professionally on stage most of my life. The scarcity of dancers in Mexico forced me to take on the role of full-time dancer as well as choreographer and director. This triple role enabled me to understand the hardship of a dancer's life. Since my days in New York, I'd seen dancers who were physically destroyed because of lack of proper nutrition in order to conform with some impossible aesthetic dream, or who never had the chance to have a family, or who had children, and as a result were fired from ballet companies. All these considerations gave me a different approach to dancers. I believe that dancers must be viewed not just as the tools of a choreographer but as human beings. Dancers should lead full lives and have children. The aesthetic pursuit should never hurt the health of a dancer. No intellectual or artistic criterion is valid if it implies the destruction of one's body.

The Choreographer

There is very little guidance on how to become a choreographer; thus many people become choreographers as an evolution or a consequence of their dancing careers. Mr. B. always opposed this approach. In that sense, I was very fortunate to have received his ideas not only as a dancer but also as a choreographer. I don't believe that people who have danced all their lives are necessarily able to become choreographers. Some of the qualities that made them good dancers—memory, the ability to recreate and to repeat—limit them when they try to invent movement. I also don't believe that someone can be a choreographer if she doesn't dance as well as or better than any of her dancers. It's very important for the choreographer to be able to demonstrate what she wants the dancers to do. The two careers must be led simultaneously. If you want to be a choreographer, you must start as early as possible.

Society

The massacre of students in Mexico in 1968, the tragic experience in Chile after the military coup of 1973, the dictatorships in other Latin American countries, and the vast poverty of my own country made me aware that dance should play a social role. The goal of making dance useful to society has led me, in the last three decades, to consistently work toward making dance accessible to all. I believe in the importance of dancing for the underdog and for the young.

My concern with using dance as a means of social expression and my need to increase the projection of the dancer led me to rehearsal techniques similar to those of acting schools such as Grotovsky's and Cintolesi's. I was concerned not only with the dancer's physique but also with his or her inner motivation. My experience as a mother also made me much more aware of human emotions. This approach brought me closer to what some people were doing in the theater and in modern dance.

In an opposite direction, in the '80s I came in contact with the Russian technique, pre-Balanchine. My experience in Russia was extremely important for me. I wrote two books on orthodox ballet methodology and I had the opportunity to stage my works in St. Petersburg and enrich them by using Russian dancers in them.

Conclusion

My incorporation of contemporary acting techniques as well as modern and popular dance, and my exploration of traditional ballet are not really departures from George Balanchine's ideas. He believed in maintaining the ballet tradition but opening it up to evolution. Like him, I believe that innovation comes from tradition. These two elements are the cornerstone of Mr. B.'s legacy, as well as Stravinsky's and Picasso's, which, put succinctly, affirm that you can only break the rules if you know them very well.

The last time I saw Mr. B. was in 1983. I wrote him a letter that never reached him and I went to see him in the hospital. My son, Gregorio, had a marionette of a ballerina. I looked at Mr. B. He held my hand, but I couldn't fully grasp what he was telling me. He said something about time. I felt a connection then; when we showed him the marionette, he held it. My son tried to get him to sign it, but he had a very difficult time doing this. He remarked, "She has short legs."

As important as his technical recommendations were, the fundamental thing I learned from Balanchine is that dance is art. It is a religion, a spiritual commitment that you do not sell, a form of prayer, a form of communion, a way of bringing people together and taking them to a higher level.

Index of Names

Diana Adams (1926–1993): A dancer with American Ballet Theatre who became a principal dancer with the New York City Ballet and later taught at the School of American Ballet.

Alvin Ailey (1931–1989): A major American dancer, choreographer, and director. Ailey studied with Lester Horton, Martha Graham and others; performed on Broadway; and, in 1958, founded the now world-famous Alvin Ailey Dance Company, which devotes itself to preserving and enhancing the American dance tradition and to celebrating black cultural expression. Alvin Ailey created 79 ballets, including his masterpiece, *Revelations*.

Alicia Alonso (b. 1920): A Cuban ballerina and director who has become a legend in her time. After studies in Havana and at the School of American Ballet, she earned international renown for her portrayals of "Giselle" and "Carmen." In 1948, she founded her own company, renamed after the Revolution as the National Ballet of Cuba. Alonso has suffered from a congenital near-blindness throughout her life.

American Ballet Theatre: One of the most important ballet companies of the Twentieth Century, founded in 1937 as the Mordkin Ballet, reorganized in 1940 as the Ballet Theatre—its first performance was at Radio City Music Hall in 1941—and given its present name in 1956. ABT resides at the Metropolitan Opera House in New York.

George Balanchine (1904–1983): Widely recognized as one of the greatest choreographers in the history of ballet. The Russian-born dancer and choreographer founded the School of American Ballet in 1934 and, with Lincoln Kirstein, the Ballet Society, in 1946—renamed as the New York City Ballet in 1948. Among his many ballets are *Agon*, *Apollo*, *The Firebird*, *Orpheus* (music by Stravinsky), *Serenade*, and *Seven Deadly Sins* (music by Kurt Weill, text by Bertolt Brecht).

Bolshoi Ballet: Russia's leading ballet company, known for elaborate productions that preserve classical dance traditions. Among its repertory are Tchaikovsky's *Swan Lake* and *The Nutcracker* and

Prokofiev's *Romeo and Juliet*. During the Soviet era, the company's extensive international touring enhanced its profile in the West. Gloria Contreras saw performances by the Bolshoi in New York that featured Galina Ulanova, Maya Plistetskaya, and others.

Gordon Boelzner (1937–2005): The accompanist for rehearsals of Contreras's *Ocho por radio*. Boelzner later became musical director, pianist, and conductor for the New York City Ballet.

Erik Bruhn (1929–1986): A Danish ballet dancer acclaimed worldwide in his time. Bruhn was known for his roles in ballets including *La Sylphide*, *Giselle*, and *Swan Lake*. He served as a guest artist and director with companies including American Ballet Theatre.

Jorge Cano: A dancer in the Mexican premier of Contreras's *Huapango* at Mexico's Palacio de Bellas Artes in 1959. He later performed with various companies in Cuba and Mexico, and served as ballet master at the Compañía Nacional Clásica, Mexico's national ballet company.

Ana Cardús (b. 1943): A student of Nelsy Dambré who danced in Contreras's *Huapango* in Mexico City in 1959. She performed with various international ballet companies and later settled in Switzerland.

Carlos Chávez (1899–1978): One of Mexico's musical giants and a major twentieth-century composer. His principal works, among them symphonies, ballets, and pieces for voice, include *Sinfonía de Antígona*, *Sinfonía índia*, and *La hija de Cólquide*, (written for Martha Graham).

Margarita Contreras (b. 1943): A dancer, choreographer, and teacher as well as the author's sister. Since 1970, she has served as artistic consultant for the Taller Coreográfico de la UNAM.

Birgit Cullberg (1908–1999): A Swedish dancer, choreographer, and director who was a member of the Royal Ballet of London and later founded the Cullberg Ballet in Sweden. Cullberg enjoyed an international reputation for her experimental choreography.

Nelsy Dambré (1908–1976): A French-born dancer who performed with the Paris Opera as well as with other European companies before settling in Mexico, where she became a pioneer of classical ballet. Madame Dambré instructed Contreras, Lupe Serrano, and many other dancers.

Kenneth Dewey: A member of a prominent U.S. family—his grandfather, Thomas E. Dewey, ran for president in 1948—who was a guest at Columbia University's International House during Contreras's association there.

Peter Dickinson (b. 1934): A British musician, composer, and teacher. Dickinson composed the music for Contreras's *Vitálitas*.

Felia Doubrovska (1896–1981). A Russian dancer who studied at the Imperial Academy of St. Petersburg, and later was an instructor at the School of American Ballet; Contreras studied with her there.

Rosemary Dunleavy: A student at the School of American Ballet who became a member of the New York City Ballet. She danced in the Gloria Contreras Dance Company.

Bill Earl: A student at the School of American Ballet who later danced with Contreras's México Lindo company and the New York City Ballet.

André Egelvsky (1917–1977): Considered the greatest male classical dancer of his generation. Egelvsky trained in France, danced with the Ballet Russe de Monte Carlo, and became premier *danseur* for the New York City Ballet (1951–58).

El mercado [**The Market**]: Contreras's first choreographed piece (1958), set to Blas Galindo's *Sones de mariachi* (1940) in a version using 19 mariachi musicians. It premiered in New York and in Mexico City; its Mexico premiere at the Palacio de Bellas Artes featured performances by Contreras, her sister Margarita, and Silvia Ramírez.

Judith Friedman: A dancer who studied at the School of American Ballet and performed with Contreras's México Lindo company—particularly in the New York production of *El mercado*—and with the New York City Ballet. She also earned acclaim as a pianist.

Blas Galindo (1910–1993): A Mexican musician, composer, and conductor. Among his more than 150 compositions—orchestral and vocal works, chamber music, and solo piano-pieces—is his *Sones de mariachi* (1940), from which Contreras choreographed her piece *El mercado* (1958).

Tamara Geva (1906?–1997): A Russian ballerina who danced with the Ballets Russes and the Soviet State Dancers, married George Balanchine—with whom she emigrated to the United States in 1924—and later performed in Broadway musicals and in films.

Martha Graham (1894–1991): The American dancer, choreographer, and teacher widely considered the greatest innovator of modern dance. She founded the now world-renowned Martha Graham Dance Company in 1926. Among Graham's numerous pieces, many of which she performed and which employ classical myths or seminal texts, are *Appalachian Spring* (music by Copland), *Clytemnestra*, *Lamentation*, and *Letter to the World*.

Melissa Hayden (1923–2006): A Canadian-born ballerina who was a principal dancer with the New York City Ballet.

Barbara Horgan: George Balanchine's personal assistant (1962–1983), presently Chairman of the Board of Directors of The George Balanchine Foundation and Trustee-General Director of The George Balanchine Trust.

Huapango: Contreras's signature work (1958), set to music by José Pablo Moncayo. It premiered in New York in 1958 and in Mexico City in February 1959 at the Palacio de Bellas Artes; the latter performance, by the Ballet Concierto, was directed by Felipe Segura.

Jacob's Pillow: The Berkshires property purchased in 1930 by dancer/choreographer Ted Shawn. It was first used for a summer theater, later for the headquarters for Shawn's dance company, then for the now-famous dance festival that Shawn directed. Contreras premiered her piece *The Wise and Foolish Virgins* [Parable] here in 1959.

Robert Joffrey (1930–1988): A major American dancer, choreographer, and director. Joffrey studied at the School of American Ballet and the High School of Performing Arts, and in 1956 founded the Joffrey Ballet. The company earned acclaim in the 1960s for its innovative approach to ballet and today is considered one of the most important dance companies in the United States.

Allegra Kent (b. 1937): An American dancer who studied with Bronislava Nijinska and at the School of American Ballet. She was a principal dancer with the New York City Ballet.

Lincoln Kirstein (1907–1996): With George Balanchine and Edward Warburg, he founded the School of American Ballet (1933); and, with Balanchine, the Ballet Society (1946), renamed the New York City Ballet (1948). Kirstein commissioned and helped fund the New York State Theater, the home of the NYCB. He served as the company's general director (1948–1989). He wrote extensively on dance and art.

Nancy Lassalle: A friend and colleague of Lincoln Kirstein, a director emerita at the New York City Ballet, and the secretary of the board of the School of American Ballet.

Loi Leabo: An American dancer who was a student at the Metropolitan Opera ballet school and a member of Contreras's México Lindo company.

Tanaquil LeClercq (1929–2000): One of the most celebrated ballerinas of the New York City Ballet. Born in Paris, LeClercq studied at the School of American Ballet before her tenure at the NYCB. In 1956, while on tour in Europe, she contracted polio, which tragically ended her career. She was married to Balanchine from 1952 to 1969.

Nicholas Magallanes (1922–1977): One of the earliest principal dancers with the New York City Ballet. The Mexican-born Magallanes earned renown for his performance in the title role of Balanchine's *Orpheus*.

Eduardo Mata (1942–1995): A leading Mexican composer whose works include symphonies, chamber-works, and sonatas. In addition to composing, Mata also conducted the UNAM Philharmonic and the Guadalajara Orchestra.

Patricia McBride (b. 1942): A student at the School of American Ballet who joined the New York City Ballet in 1959 and became a principal dancer there.

Marlene Mesavage (b. 1940): A student at the School of American Ballet who danced with Contreras's México Lindo company—particularly in the New York production of *El mercado*—and with the New York City Ballet.

Veronika Mlakar (b. 1935): A Zurich-born dancer who performed in various companies in Europe and the United States, including the American Ballet Theatre. She performed the principal role in *Vitálitas* with the Gloria Contreras Dance Company.

Igor Moiseyev (1906–2007): Considered the greatest twentieth-century choreographer of folk dance. Born in Kiev, Moiseyev studied at, danced with, and choreographed for the Bolshoi Ballet. He later became director of the folk dance company that bears his name.

José Pablo Moncayo (1912–1958): A Mexican composer whose works include orchestral pieces, operas, and ballets. His most famous piece, *Huapango* (1941), inspired Contreras's ballet of the same title, which premiered in 1959.

Carlos Navarro (1906–1984): An acclaimed Mexican actor who starred in films including *Doña Perfecta* (starring Dolores del Río), *The Brave One*, and *Illusion Travels by Streetcar*.

Pascual Navarro: A Mexican doctor who was also an outstanding guitarist and singer.

New York City Ballet: The world-famous ballet company founded by George Balanchine and Lincoln Kirstein. Originally named the Ballet Society (1946), the company was renamed in 1948 when it was relocated to the New York City Center of Music and Drama. In 1964, it moved to the New York State Theater at Lincoln Center, where it presently resides. The ballet company's hallmark has been its combination of European tradition with American innovation.

Anatole Oboukhoff (1896–1962): A Russian-born dancer and instructor who studied at the Imperial School of St. Petersburg and later taught at the School of American Ballet. He was considered one of the best dancers of his time.

Ocho por radio **[Eight for Radio]**: One of Contreras's early pieces, choreographed to Silvestre Revueltas's 1933 composition by the same title. The piece premiered in "Panamerica" in January 1960, performed by the New York City Ballet.

"Panamerica": A performance by the New York City Ballet in January 1960, conceived by Balanchine and Kirstein and organized by Carlos Chávez. The event featured premieres of works choreographed by Balanchine, Monción, and Contreras set to music by Latin American composers including Chávez, Revueltas, and Villa-Lobos.

Janet Reed (1916–2000): A lively dancer, known for her leaps, who performed in various companies, including the San Francisco Ballet and the New York City Ballet. She served as ballet mistress at the NYCB from 1959 to 1964.

Silvestre Revueltas (1899–1940): A major Mexican composer, violinist, and conductor. His works include orchestral works, chamber music, ballets, and film scores. His *Ocho por radio* (1933) inspired Contreras's piece of the same name.

Jerome Robbins (1918–1998): A dancer and major choreographer of ballets, Broadway musicals, and films, among them *Fancy Free*, *West-Side Story*, and *Fiddler on the Roof*. Robbins won four Tony Awards and two Academy Awards. At the invitation of George Balanchine, he joined the New York City Ballet as a dancer, choreographer, and associate director from 1949 to 1959; he later served as its ballet master.

School of American Ballet: The world-famous school founded in 1934 by Lincoln Kirstein, George Balanchine, Vladimir Dimitriev, and Edward Warburg. Now the official school of the New York City Ballet, located in the Juilliard Building at Lincoln Center. Its most prominent instructors have included Danilova, Doubrovska, Stuart, Egelvsky, and Oboukhoff.

Felipe Segura: A Mexican dancer, choreographer, and director who performed with various companies in Mexico and Cuba. Segura served as a principal dancer as well as artistic director at the Ballet Concierto de México. He directed the company during the Mexican premier of Contreras's *Huapango* in 1959.

Lupe Serrano (b. 1930): A student of Nelsy Dambré in Mexico—she was Contreras's classmate—who became a principal dancer with American Ballet Theatre and an instructor at the Washington Ballet.

Ted Shawn (1891–1972): A renowned American dancer, choreographer, and instructor. With Ruth St. Denis, he founded the Denishawn Company in 1915, considered a cornerstone of American dance. He later bought the Berkshires property that became Jacob's Pillow, the renowned dance festival.

Joysanne Sidimus: A student at the School of American Ballet who danced with the Gloria Contreras Dance Company and the New York City Ballet.

Igor Stravinsky (1882–1971): One of the greatest composers of the twentieth century and the one who most influenced ballet. George Balanchine choreographed pieces to Stravinsky's *The Firebird* and *Orpheus*, among others.

Muriel Stuart (1901–1991): An English-born ballerina who danced with Pavlova in her youth and later distinguished herself as a teacher at the School of American Ballet. She was co-author, with Lincoln Kirstein, of a seminal book on classical ballet.

Carol Sumner: A student at the School of American Ballet who later danced in the Gloria Contreras Dance Company and as a principal dancer with the New York City Ballet.

Paul Taylor (b. 1930): A major American choreographer. In his youth Taylor danced in Martha Graham's and Merce Cunningham's companies as well as in the New York City Ballet. In 1954 he founded the now renowned Paul Taylor Dance Company, known for its cutting-edge choreography and controversial themes.

Ethel Thurston (1912–2006): A U.S. musicologist of Medieval and Renaissance music who was Contreras's music instructor for several years. Thurston was also a pioneer of the animal rights movement.

Carola Trier (1913–2000): A German survivor of World War Two who emigrated to the United States, where she danced and performed acrobatics on skates. After studying with Joseph Pilates, she applied his method to numerous dancers in the New York City Ballet. Trier taught as well as sponsored Contreras during her New York period.

Violette Verdy (b. 1933): A French-born ballerina who became a principal dancer with the New York City Ballet and later directed the Paris Opera Ballet.

Esther Villavicencio: A Cuban ballerina who was a member of Contreras's México Lindo company—she performed in the New York production of *El mercado*—and the Chicago Ballet.

Vitálitas: Contreras's 1959 ballet, choreographed to music by British composer Peter Dickinson. It premiered in New York that same year, and in Mexico in 1960. It has subsequently been performed by the Joffrey Ballet in New York and by other companies in Chicago and Brazil.

Patricia Wilde (b. 1928): A Canadian-born dancer who was the first *danseur* of the New York City Ballet.

The Wise and Foolish Virgins [Parable]: An early piece by Contreras (1959), choreographed from a twelfth-century anonymous composition based on a biblical parable. Her group premiered it at Jacob's Pillow in 1959.

Alek Zybine: A Mexican dancer who studied with the Ballet Russe de Monte Carlo and performed as a soloist for the Metropolitan Opera Ballet. He danced with Contreras's México Lindo in New York.

Photographs

Gloria Contreras. *Huapango* (rehearsal), Ballet Concierto salon, Mexico City, 1959. Photograph by José Luis Arreguín.

Left to right (foreground): Gloria Contreras, Bill Earl. *Huapango*, Kaufmann Concert Hall, New York, 1962.

Gloria Contreras. *Huapango* (rehearsal), Academia de la Danza Mexicana rooftop, Mexico City, 1959.

Left to right: Esther Villavicencio, Gloria Contreras, Judith Friedman. *El mercado*, México Lindo company, International House, New York, 1958.

Left to right: Gloria Contreras, Pascual Navarro. México Lindo company,
International House, New York, 1958.

John Wittenberg. *El mercado*, México Lindo company, International House, New York, 1958.

Marlene Mesavage. *El mercado*, México Lindo company, International House, New York, 1958. Photograph © Martha Swope.

Left to right: Esther Villavicencio, Gloria Contreras, Judith Friedman.
El mercado, México Lindo company, International House, New York, 1958.

Marlene Mesavage (center). *The Wise and Foolish Virgins*, Kaufmann Concert
Hall, New York, 1962. Photograph © Martha Swope.

Thomas Enckell (standing) with Margarita Contreras, Gloria Contreras, Julie Rigler, Penelope Gates, Margot Yanitelli, and Judy Lowenthal. *Vitálitas*, Kaufmann Concert Hall, New York, 1962. Photograph © Martha Swope.

Front-center, rear-center: Jillana, Arthur Mitchell. *Ocho por radio*, New York City Ballet, New York, 1960. Photograph © Martha Swope.

Left to right: Bill Earl, Allegra Kent, William Weslow. *Serenata Concertante*, "Panamerica," New York City Ballet, New York, 1960.

Gloria Contreras (center) with dancers of Gloria Contreras Dance Company
(second period). *Danzas*, New York, 1967.

Left to right: Karen Williamson, Gloria Contreras. Gloria Contreras Dance Company (second period), 5 Great Jones Street, New York, 1967.

Gloria Contreras and students (Karen Williamson, Gerrie Paige, Shirley
Oakes, Linda Garner). Gloria Contreras Dance Company (second period),
5 Great Jones Street, New York, 1967.

Gloria Contreras (center) with dancers of Gloria Contreras Dance Company (second period), New York, 1967.

Gloria Contreras. *Danza para mujeres* [Dance for Women], Mexico City, 1970. Photograph by Lourdes Almeida.

Gloria Contreras Dance Company (second period). *Eioua*, Kaufmann
Concert Hall, New York, 1967. Photograph © Martha Swope.

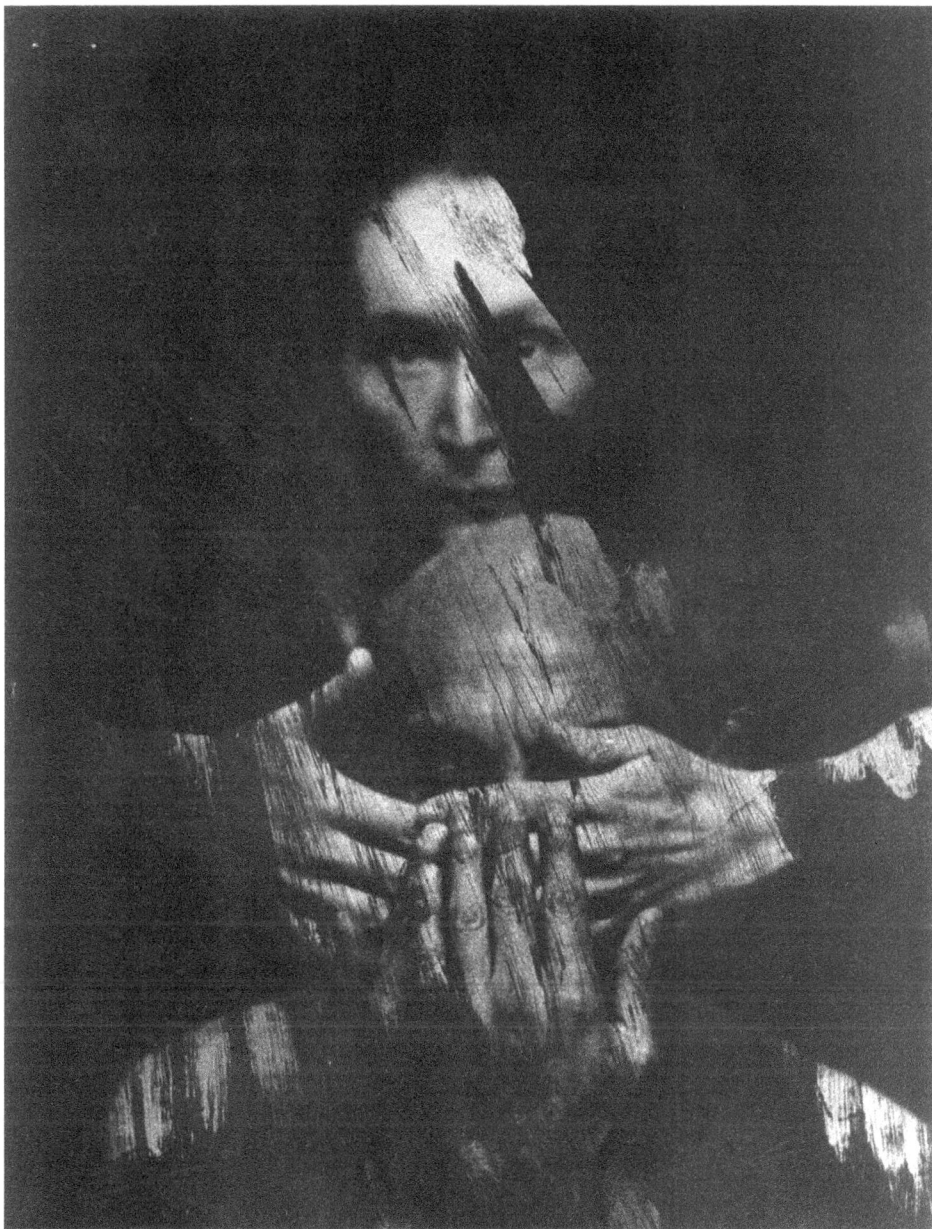

Gloria Contreras with Patricio Bunster. *Calaucán*, Taller Coreográfico de la UNAM, Sala Miguel Covarrubias, Mexico City, 1980. Photograph by José Murguía.

Gloria Contreras. *Galileo*, Taller Coreográfico de la UNAM, Mexico City, 2008. Photograph by Gabriel Eduardo.

In this photo, Contreras, at 73 years of age, dancing the lead role in her latest ballet, demonstrates that "dancers aren't ephemeral. All that's necessary is to keep working." (GC)

Appendices

Appendix A

Fourteen Lessons from George Balanchine

1. A choreographer should always know more than her dancers so she will be able to lift them to higher levels.

2. Music is the heart of a dance. A choreographer must know this art professionally so she can analyze the works and not only use the most obvious part (the melody) but all of its structural elements.

3. Knowledge of the plastic arts is also necessary because each moment of a dance should be a perfect picture. A choreographer should have an understanding of sculpture, from the most ancient to the most modern.

4. He used to speak about creating a "handicap" in the construction of every dance. He told me never to accept the first ideas that come to mind, but to struggle and explore inside myself in order to reach new discoveries.

5. He advised me to avoid perfect dancers because they make it easy for the choreographer to resolve a problem without having to think it through. If a dancer isn't perfect or beautiful, the choreographer will be forced to create ten ideas from which she'll be able to select one.

6. The choreographer should put herself in the position of her dancers—whether they are Jews, Latinos, or Anglo Saxons. She should create for their individual temperaments and take advantage of their respective strengths.

7. He reminded me to consider the audience: "Their presence is essential to the development and durability of a company; you must give them the kind of work from which they can extract some benefit. A ballet can offer emotion or simply beauty. Depending upon who they are, give them a highly intellectual work or one that's simple."

8. "For a ballet to be good, the dancing itself must capture attention. If you have to read a storyline or explanation to understand a ballet, it's because the dancing itself doesn't communicate."

9. He advised me not to fear "borrowing" from him ("I am your family"), and likened choreography to poetry: the poet doesn't invent words, he selects them, arranges them, gives them a rhythm, and produces images and atmosphere. "A leg is a leg and the arabesque has existed for 400 years." What matters is how one creates and interweaves movements; that determines whether or not the spectators will see something in the ballet that transforms them.

10. He recommended that I create my own language and become a choreographer for my generation. For him, choreography was a career that began when he was fifteen years old. He abhorred performers who thought that the career of choreographer was simply the culmination of a long career in dance.

11. "Create and throw away. Develop yourself through work and experience."

12. "You don't have to sell anything. Never become a salesman."

13. "Triumph lies in developing knowledge, not in money." Nevertheless, he understood that money was necessary to develop art: "To produce an *Agon*, you have to produce a *Nutcracker*."

14. "Pay attention to the opinions of one or two people in relation to your work. Don't listen to the applause or the insults. The critics have to eat, but you don't have to read them."

The above was compiled by Gloria Contreras from her personal conversations with George Balanchine; an earlier version appeared in Dance *magazine (December 1996).*

Appendix B
Author's Credo

In the Taller Coreográfico de la UNAM, I have assembled a group of dancers who believe, just as I do, that dance is a form of communication. For us, dance is more than a profession; it is a way of life that teaches a greater understanding of life itself.

Throughout my career as a dancer, I have faced both the positive and negative impact of fundamentally classical training. By classical, I mean the language of ballet developed over the years with the collaboration of many artists and teachers in different countries.

That academic foundation makes it possible to model the body, imbue it with movement and harmony. Well-taught and well-assimilated, it allows the dancer to feel natural even when executing the most sophisticated movements.

However, at the same time it is possible that this very discipline does not encourage the development of individuality in dancers. On many occasions, children studying dance are intensively and continuously subjected to this technique. When they emerge from this training during adolescence, they often have not achieved individual personalities as dancers and their creative spirit has been crushed.

In order to avoid these pitfalls, I believe that the notion of play must be kept alive in teaching dance. In addition to receiving technical training, the student should learn how to improvise to music, sing, play rhythms, and imitate animals, plants, and the elements. S/he should learn how to stimulate joy within and be able to concentrate on a serious theme. The pupil should learn mental discipline and be allowed to break the rules once s/he learns and knows how to execute them perfectly.

Technique should not be always taught within the four walls of a studio. Some of the instruction should be conducted in the open air. The dancer must grow in contact with nature, never isolated from it.

The dancer should understand the importance of blood circulation and oxygen control; understanding their relationship will help the dancer preserve a clear vision of what s/he receives from the outside and what s/he draws from within.

Improvisation brings life to gestures and makes a dance complete, penetrating to the deepest fibers of one's being; it frees facial and corporeal expressions. It is the first step in choreography. A dancer must be capable of dancing without borrowed gestures, of inventing her/his own, and of maintaining innate spontaneity. A dancer must realize that s/he possesses a body that is a finely tuned instrument which has been subjected to a technique but which also is a means of self-expression, not an obstacle to its development.

When a dancer decides to becomes a choreographer, s/he must possess absolute control of her/his body and an adventurous mind that whole-heartedly enjoys experimentation. Based on my experience with the creative process, this cannot be developed *a priori* but requires an understanding of music, painting, and history before one confronts the demands of choreographing works.

To create, the choreographer must come face to face with her/his dancers and the score. S/he interweaves a structure, beginning with an idea of movement which is then developed by exploiting the potential of that idea. At times, composition is linear, at others times, non-linear, producing scenarios within a scenario that proliferate into different worlds that possess individual value but which also interplay to produce the structure of a whole.

At the same time that an intellectual composition is developed from movement, an aesthetic begins to take shape that in turn is suffused with an emotionally charged atmosphere. The structure of a work will come to life only when the dancers interpreting it are true artists, not mere gymnasts.

I believe that an artistic dancer is someone who is in full control of the self, who can use this sense of self as a full collaborator in the artistic product through control of one's vanity and the destructive forces in dance. A true dancer is someone who is absolutely sincere in her/his life, and who as a consequence turns to dance, and dances in order to give and to receive what other human beings emanate.

Through my choreography, and more concretely within my activity as director of the Taller Coreográfico de la UNAM, I've wanted to return to dance itself, eliminating everything about it that might weaken it. I've avoided following literary plots as well as exaggerated theatrical effects. I've tried to make my works valid, even naked. I've preserved sound and color, leaving the dancer with the mission of expressing everything without any external help.

Dance transmits emotions; it refutes, disturbs, and soothes. Choreography may be an intellectual game, an aesthetic pleasure, a means of finding the soul, or a bitter reproof. It is strength against alienation. The Taller Coreográfico de la UNAM strives to give itself to its audience, while discovering itself in the process.

Appendix C

Gloria Contreras's Choreographed Works

Premiere	Ballet	Length	Music	Year
Nueva York	*Huapango*	8′ 32″	José Pablo Moncayo	1958
Nueva York	*El mercado* [The Market]	6′ 45″	Blas Galindo	1958
Nueva York	*The Wise and Foolish Virgins*		Música anónima del siglo XII	1959
Nueva York	*Vitálitas*	13′ 35″	Peter Dickinson	1959
Nueva York	*Serenata concertante*	30′	Juan Orrego Salas	1960
Nueva York	*Ocho por radio* [8 for Radio]	6′	Silvestre Revueltas	1960
Nueva York	*Alusiones* [Allusions]	20′	Anton von Webern	1960
Nueva York	*Planos*	9′	Silvestre Revueltas	1962
Nueva York	*Eioua*	12′ 10″	Guillaume de Machaut	1962
Nueva York	*Sensemayá*	7′	Silvestre Revueltas	1965
Nueva York	*Sonata para piano* [Sonata for Piano]	11′	Igor Stravinsky	1966
Brasil	*Concierto en re (1er. movimiento)* [Concerto in D (1st movement)]	10′	Johann Sebastian Bach	1967
Brasil	*Divertimento*		Edino Krieger	1967
Nueva York	*La muerte de un cazador* [Death of a Hunter]	12′	Gustav Mahler	1967
México	*Ludio*		José Antonio Alcaraz	1967
Nueva York	*Danzas* [Dances]		Rodolfo Halffter	1967
Nueva York	*Adagio y Allegro* [Adagio and Allegro]	15′	Johann Sebastian Bach	1967
Nueva York	*Diana y Acteón*	10′	Rodin de Boismortier	1967
Nueva York	*Isostasia*	8′ 40″	Eduardo Mata	1968
Nueva York	*Aguafuerte* [Etching]	25′	Gustavo Becerra	1969
Nueva York	*Opus 32*	10′	Bruno Maderna	1969

Premiere	Ballet	Length	Music	Year
Nueva York	*Danza para mujeres* [Dance for Women]	20′ 45″	Giovanni Battista Pergolesi	1970
Nueva York	*Interludia* [Interlude]	6′ 13″	Hans Werner Henze	1970
México, UNAM *	*Los muertos en la plaza (Integrales)* [The Dead in the Plaza (Intégrales)]	9′ 41″	Edgard Varèse	1971
México, UNAM *	*Cantábile*	19′ 33″	Piotr I. Tchaikovsky	1971
México, UNAM *	*Cantos de Maldoror* [Songs of Maldoror]	45′	Poemas de Lautreamont	1971
México, UNAM *	*Electrodanzable*	8′ 45″	Manuel Enríquez	1972
México, UNAM *	*A dos* [Duet]	11′ 15″	Manuel Enríquez	1972
México, UNAM *	*Adagio y fuga* [Adagio and Fugue]	8′ 22″	Wolfgang A. Mozart	1972
México, UNAM *	*Jazzotomía*	7′ 25″	Juan José Calatayud	1973
México, UNAM *	Ocho por jazz [Eight for Jazz]	14′ 50″	Dave Brubeck	1973
México, UNAM *	*Sinfonía* [Symphony]	10′ 06″	Igor Stravinsky	1974
México, UNAM *	*Canticum Sacrum*	17′ 13″	Igor Stravinsky	1974
México, UNAM *	*Tres* [Three]	9′ 23″	Mario Lavista	1975
México, UNAM *	*Arcana*	11′ 33″	Edgard Varése	1975
México, UNAM *	*Continuum*	3′	Gyorgy Ligeti	1976
México, UNAM *	*Hora de junio* [Hour of June]	11′	Silvestre Revueltas	1976
México, UNAM *	*Cuarteto en fa* [Quartet in F]	26′	Maurice Ravel	1977
México, UNAM *	*Réquiem para un poeta* [Requiem for a Poet]	14′ 27″	Igor Stravinsky	1977
México, UNAM *	*Tempos bachianos*	15′ 20″	Johann Sebastian Bach	1978
México, UNAM *	*Leidenschaft* [Passion]	16′ 50″	Alban Berg	1978

Premiere	Ballet	Length	Music	Year
México, UNAM *	*Concierto en re (nueva versión)*	24′ 32′′	Johann Sebastian Bach	1978
La Habana, Cuba	*Gravitacional* [Gravitational]		Mario Lavista	1978
México, UNAM *	*Redivivo* [Revived]	5′ 45′′	Carlos Malcolm	1979
México, UNAM *	*Sonata para chelo y piano* [Sonata for Cello and Piano]	12′	Claude A. Debussy	1979
México, UNAM *	*Besos (Opus 45)* [Kisses (Opus 45)]	19′ 15′′	Berg/Segovia (poesía)	1979
México, UNAM *	*Ofrenda* [Offering]	19′ 20′′	Johann Sebastian Bach	1980
México, UNAM *	*Ionización* [Ionization]	4′	Edgard Varèse	1980
México, UNAM *	*Sensemayá (nueva versión)*	7′	Silvestre Revueltas	1980
México, UNAM *	*Cuarteto en sol* [Quartet in G]	26′	Claude A. Debussy	1980
México, UNAM *	*Sinfonía de los salmos* [Symphony of Psalms]	20′ 20′′	Igor Stravinsky	1981
México, UNAM *	*Alusiones (nueva versión)*	20′	Anton von Webern	1981
México, UNAM *	*Concierto para violín y orquesta* [Concerto for Violin and Orchestra]	21′ 28′′	Igor Stravinsky	1981
México, UNAM *	*Planos (nueva versión)*	9′	Silvestre Revueltas	1982
México, UNAM *	*Cuatro danzas mexicanas* [Four Mexican Dances]	4′	Manuel M. Ponce	1982
México, UNAM *	*Octandre*	6′ 47′′	Edgard Varèse	1983
México, UNAM *	*El califas* [The Caliph]	3′ 11′′	Igor Stravinsky	1983
México, UNAM *	*La ronda* [The Round]	4′ 20′′	Leonardo Velázquez	1983
México, UNAM *	*Una pierna para Neruda* [A Leg for Neruda]	20′	Dimitri Shostakovitch	1983
México, UNAM *	*La caída de los ángeles* [The Fall of the Angels]	12′	Federico Ibarra	1983
México, UNAM *	*Cuarteto opus 135*	25′	Ludwig van Beethoven	1984

Premiere	Ballet	Length	Music	Year
México, UNAM *	*Homenaje a Balanchine* [Homage to Balanchine]	24´ 50´´	Igor Stravinsky	1984
México, UNAM *	*Imágenes del Quinto Sol* [Images from the Fifth Sun]	26´ 40´´	Federico Ibarra	1984
México, UNAM *	*Juana de Arco en la hoguera* [Joan of Arc at the Stake]	2 horas	Arthur Honegger	1984
México, UNAM *	*Ofrenda musical* [Musical Offering]	18´ 26´´	Johann Sebastian Bach	1985
México, UNAM *	*Un laurel para ti* [A Laurel for You]	15´	Silvestre Revueltas	1985
México, UNAM *	*Carmen. Dos danzas de amor* [. . . Two Dances of Love]	4´ 50´´	Georges Bizet	1985
México, UNAM *	*Concierto para piano y orquesta* [Concerto for Piano and Orchestra]	19´ 26´´	Maurice Ravel	1986
México, UNAM *	*El mar* [The Sea]	23´	Claude A. Debussy	1986
México, UNAM *	*Claro de luna* [Claire de Lune]	16´	Claude A. Debussy	1987
México, UNAM *	*Alabanzas* [Praises]	19´ 06´´	Leonard Bernstein	1987
México, UNAM *	*Isadora*	6´ 45´´	Beethoven/Wagner	1987
México, UNAM *	*Dvorak*	25´	Antonin Dvorak	1988
México, UNAM *	*Marsias*	8´ 50´´	Mario Lavista	1988
México, UNAM *	*Danzas sacra y profana* [Sacred and Secular Dances]	10´ 51´´	Claude A. Debussy	1988
México, UNAM *	*Noche de encantamiento* [Night of Enchantment]	9´ 50´´	Silvestre Revueltas	1989
México, UNAM *	*Trío para piano* [Piano Trio]	29´	Maurice Ravel	1989
México, UNAM *	*Bachiana*	6´ 04´´	Heitor Villa-Lobos	1989
México, UNAM *	*Sonata para violín y violonchelo* [Sonata for Violin and Violoncello]	19´	Maurice Ravel	1989
México, UNAM *	*La siesta de un fauno* [A Faun's Nap]	9´ 05´´	Claude A. Debussy	1989
México, UNAM *	*Magnificat*	26´	Johann Sebastian Bach	1990

Premiere	Ballet	Length	Music	Year
México, UNAM *	*Divertimento*	24´	Igor Stravinsky	1990
México, UNAM *	*Intermezzo*	3´	Manuel M. Ponce	1991
México, UNAM *	*Adagio K.622*	7´ 39´´	Wolfgang A. Mozart	1991
México, UNAM *	*Cuarteto KV.465 (de las disonancias)* [Dissonance Quartet]	25´	Wolfgang A. Mozart	1991
México, UNAM *	*Danzas concertantes*	20´	Igor Stravinsky	1991
México, UNAM *	*Brandenburgo núm. 3* [Brandenberg no. 3]	11´	Johann Sebastian Bach	1991
México, UNAM *	*Concierto para cuerdas y metales* [Concerto for Strings and Brass]	17´	Paul Hindemith	1992
México, UNAM *	*L'estro armónico*	30´	Antonio Vivaldi	1992
México, UNAM *	*Resurrexit*	4´	Johann Sebastian Bach	1992
México, UNAM *	*Alaya*	14´	Béla Bartók	1992
México, UNAM *	*Danzas para cuerdas, percusiones y celesta* [Dances for Strings, Percussion, and Celeste]	15´	Béla Bartók	1992
México, UNAM *	*Alaíde*	6´	Sergei Rachmaninoff	1992
México, UNAM *	*Romeo y Julieta* [Romeo and Juliet]	20´	Piotr I. Tchaikovsky	1993
México, UNAM *	*Réquiem de Mozart* [Mozart Requiem]	30´	Wolfgang A. Mozart	1993
México, UNAM *	*Piezas mexicanas* [Mexican Pieces]	7´ 33´´	Manuel M. Ponce	1993
México, UNAM *	*Suite N° 2 para pequeña orquesta* [. . . for Chamber Orchestra]	6´	Igor Stravinsky	1993
México, UNAM *	*Dumbarton Oaks*	14´	Igor Stravinsky	1993
México, UNAM *	*Tempo di tango*	4´	Igor Stravinsky	1993
México, UNAM *	*Rapsodia en azul* [Rhapsody in Blue]	16´ 26´´	George Gershwin	1993

Premiere	Ballet	Length	Music	Year
México, UNAM *	*Sólo para un ángel contemporáneo* [Solo for a Contemporary Angel]	4′ 29′′	Sergei Rachmaninoff	1993
México, UNAM *	*Fanfarria* [Fanfare]	4′ 13′′	John Adams	1993
México, UNAM *	*La consagración de la primavera* [The Rite of Spring]	32′	Igor Stravinsky	1994
México, UNAM *	*Concierto para piano y alientos* [Concerto for Piano and Wind Instruments]	21′	Igor Stravinsky	1994
México, UNAM *	*Danzas para los niños muertos* [Dances for the Dead Children]	30′	Gustav Mahler	1994
México, UNAM *	*Gloria*	2′ 10′′	Joseph Haydn	1995
México, UNAM *	*Credo*	3′ 41′′	Johann Sebastian Bach	1995
México, UNAM *	*Salmos primarios* [Primary Psalms]	10′	Roberto López Moreno (poesía)	1995
México, UNAM *	*Pájaro de fuego* [Firebird]	43′	Igor Stravinsky	1995
México, UNAM *	*Égloga* [Eclogue]	4′ 18′′	Leonardo Velázquez	1995
México, UNAM *	*Club verde* [Green Club]	4′ 37′′	Rodolfo Campodónico	1995
México, UNAM *	*Muerte sin fin* [Endless Death]	20′ 04′′	Richard Wagner	1995
México, UNAM *	*Souvenir*	35′	Piotr I. Tchaikovsky	1995
México, UNAM *	*Guantanamera*	15′	Jorge Córdoba	1995
México, UNAM *	*La hija pródiga* [The Prodigal Daughter]	16′	César Franck	1996
México, UNAM *	*Danzantes* [Dancers]	12′	Igor Stravinsky	1996
México, UNAM *	*Magdalena*	3′ 21′′	Hugo Wolf	1996
México, UNAM *	*Vals triste* [Sad Waltz]	6′ 04′′	Jean Sibelius	1996
México, UNAM *	*Siciliana*	2′ 34′′	Johann Sebastian Bach	1996

Premiere	Ballet	Length	Music	Year
México, UNAM *	*Gran fuga* [Grosse Fugue]	15′	Ludwig van Beethoven	1996
México, UNAM *	*Densidad 21.5*	4′ 17′′	Edgard Varèse	1996
México, UNAM *	*Capriccio*	17′	Igor Stravinsky	1996
México, UNAM *	*Isolda* [Isolde]	7′	Richard Wagner	1997
México, UNAM *	*La Conquista (Tocata)* [The Conquest (Toccata)]	14′ 37′′	Carlos Chávez	1997
México, UNAM *	*Cuarteto Rasumofsky 3* [Razumovsky Quartet 3]	32′	Ludwig van Beethoven	1997
México, UNAM *	*Allegro enérgico*	23′ 09′′	Gustav Mahler	1997
México, UNAM *	*Sinfonía fantástica* [Symphonie Fantastique]	21′	Héctor Berlioz	1997
México, UNAM *	*Quinteto opus 163*	21′	Franz Schubert	1997
México, UNAM *	*Estudio revolucionario* [Revolutionary Etude]	2′	Frédéric Chopin	1997
México, UNAM *	*Syrinx*	2′ 50′′	Claude A. Debussy	1998
México, UNAM *	*Coral, un despertar jubiloso* [Chorale, A Jubilant Awakening]	6′	Johann Sebastian Bach	1998
México, UNAM *	*Gran Ciaccona* [Grand Chaconne]	12′ 55′′	Johann Sebastian Bach	1998
México, UNAM *	*Dueto Rasumofsky 2* [Razumovsky Duet 2]	14′ 20′′	Ludwig van Beethoven	1998
México, UNAM *	*Habanera*	2′ 47′′	Ernesto Lecuona	1998
México, UNAM *	*Ocho por radio*	5′ 29′′	Silvestre Revueltas	1998
México, UNAM *	*Redes* [Nets]	16′	Silvestre Revueltas	1998
México, UNAM *	*Octeto* [Octet]	14′ 35′′	Igor Stravinsky	1998
México, UNAM *	*Sacrificio* [Sacrifice]	16′ 30′′	Igor Stravinsky	1998
México, UNAM *	*Brioso, el pájaro azul* [Brioso, Bluebird]	4′	Igor Stravinsky	1998

Premiere	Ballet	Length	Music	Year
Sin estrenar	*El abandono* [Abandonment]	25′	Velázquez/ López Moreno (poesía)	1999
México, Coyoacán *	*La valse* [Waltz]	12′ 22″	Maurice Ravel	1999
México, Coyoacán *	*Gaspar de la noche* [Gaspar of the Night]	22′ 07″	Maurice Ravel	1999
México, Coyoacán *	*Variaciones Goldberg* [Goldberg Variations]	30′	Johann Sebastian Bach	1999
México, Coyoacán *	*Tarantela* [Tarantella]	5′ 03″	Ludwig van Beethoven	1999
México, Coyoacán *	*Cánones* [Canons]	10′	Wolfgang A. Mozart	1999
México, UNAM *	*Corranda* [Courant]	2′ 14″	Johann Sebastian Bach	2000
México, UNAM *	*Gavota* [Gavotte]	3′	Johann Sebastian Bach	2000
México, UNAM *	*Preludio* [Prelude]	3′	Johann Sebastian Bach	2000
México, UNAM *	*Redención* [Redemption]	31′	Wolfgang A. Mozart	2000
México, UNAM *	*Preludio* [Prelude]	3′	Johann Sebastian Bach	2000
México, UNAM *	*Suite núm. 1* [Suite No. 1]	4′ 28″	Igor Stravinsky	2000
México, UNAM *	*Minueto* [Minuet]	6′	Maurice Ravel	2000
México, UNAM *	*Danzón*	9′ 46″	Arturo Márquez	2000
México, UNAM *	*Blues cósmico* [Kosmic Blues]	4′ 22″	Joplin / Mekler	2000
México, UNAM *	*Divertimento SZ113*	27′	Béla Bartók	2001
México, UNAM *	*Serenata española* [Spanish Serenade]	3′	Manuel M. Ponce	2001
México, UNAM *	*Crisol* [Crucible]	8′	Anton von Webern	2001
México, UNAM *	*Ceremonias* [Ceremonies]	13′ 19″	César Franck	2001
México, UNAM *	*Airoso* [Graceful]	4′ 55″	César Franck	2001

Premiere	Ballet	Length	Music	Year
México, UNAM *	*Obsesión* [Obsession]	10´	Anton von Webern	2001
México, UNAM *	*Suite de Lecuona* [Lecuona Suite]	14´	Ernesto Lecuona	2002
México, UNAM *	*Black and blue*	20´	Sidney Bechet	2002
México, UNAM *	*Concierto en la* [Concerto in A]	13´	Johann Sebastian Bach	2002
México, UNAM *	*Cuadros de una exposición* [Pictures at an Exhibition]	32´	Modeste Mussorgsky	2002
México, UNAM *	*Elegía* [Elegy]	7´ 38´´	Béla Bartók	2003
México, UNAM *	*Concierto para orquesta* [Concerto for Orchestra]	30´ 38´´	Béla Bartók	2003
México, UNAM *	*Sonata para flauta, viola y arpa* [Sonata for Flute, Viola, Harp]	16´ 27´´	Claude A. Debussy	2003
México, UNAM *	*Suite orquestal núm. 2*	19´ 43´´	Johann Sebastian Bach	2003
México, UNAM *	*Soledad* [Solitude]	4´ 37´´	Rodolfo Campodónico	2004
México, UNAM *	*Cuarteto Rasumofsky 1* [Razumovsky Quartet 1]	38´	Ludwig van Beethoven	2004
México, UNAM *	*Juegos* [Games]	18´	Robert Schumann	2004
México, UNAM *	*Concierto para oboe, violín, cuerdas y bajo continuo* [Concerto for Oboe, Violin, Strings, and Basso Continuo]	14´	Johann Sebastian Bach	2004
México, UNAM *	*Mambo*	11´ 33´´	Dámaso Pérez Prado	2005
México, UNAM *	*Oraciones* [Prayers]	31´ 47´´	Johann Sebastian Bach	2005
México, UNAM *	*Balada latinoamericana* [Latin American Ballad]	20´ 40´´	Latinoamericana	2005
México, UNAM *	*Sonata en sol menor. Cuatro formas de amar* [Sonata in G minor: Four Kinds of Love]	22´ 46´´	Ludwig van Beethoven	2005
México, UNAM *	*Pastoral*	3´	Igor Stravinsky	2005
México, UNAM *	*Cuatro piezas* [Four Pieces]	12´ 55´´	Antonin Dvorak	2005

Premiere	Ballet	Length	Music	Year
México, UNAM *	*Rock 1*	3′	Led Zeppelin	2005
México, UNAM *	*Nereidas* [Nereids]	4′ 48′′	Amador Pérez Torres, *Dimas*	2005
México, UNAM *	*Rock 2*	1′ 59′′	Elvis Presley	2006
México, UNAM *	*Rock 3*	4′ 25′′	Elvis Presley	2006
México, UNAM *	*Concierto para piano y orquesta Nº 23* [Concerto for Piano and Orchestra no. 23]	24′	Wolfgang A. Mozart	2006
México, UNAM *	*La boda* [Wedding]	6′ 45′′	Wolfgang A. Mozart	2006
México, UNAM *	*Obertura* [Overture]	7′ 30′′	Wolfgang A. Mozart	2006
México, UNAM *	*Scherzo*	14′	Gustav Mahler	2006
México, UNAM *	*Kreisleriana*	30′	Robert Schumann	2006
México, UNAM *	*Sonata*	10′	Robert Schumann	2006
México, UNAM*	*Casi una fantasía* [Almost a Fantasy]	13′	Ludwig van Beethoven	2006
México, UNAM *	*Clarín de la selva* [Clarion in the Jungle]	4′ 32′′	Juan Quevedo	2006
México, UNAM*	*La pasión* [The Passion]	7′	Johann Sebastian Bach	2006
México, UNAM *	*Nací* [I Was Born]	3′ 43′′	Daddy Yankee	2006
México, UNAM*	*Sueño de amor* [Liebestraum]	4′	Franz Liszt	2006
México, UNAM *	*Danzas de Rachmaninof* [Rachmaninoff Dances]	18′	Sergei Rachmaninof	2006
México, UNAM *	*Contra la noche* [Against the Night]	24′	Jason Webley	2006
México, UNAM *	*Ave María*	11′ 02′′	Johann Sebastian Bach, Franz Schubert y Wofgang A. Mozart	2007
México, UNAM *	*Danzas fugadas* [Fugato Danzas]	12′	Johann Sebastian Bach	2007

Premiere	Ballet	Length	Music	Year
México, UNAM *	*Give Peace a Chance*	18′ 21′′	The Beatles y John Lennon	2007
México, UNAM *	*Danza para Fernando* [Dance for Fernando]	3′ 30′′	Espiritual negro	2007
México, UNAM *	*Amargura* [Bitterness]	3′ 30′′	Manuel M. Ponce	2007
México, UNAM *	*Rompe* [Break]	3′	Daddy Yankee	2007
México, UNAM *	*Mojado* [Wet]	4′ 30′′	Ricardo Arjona/ Intocable	2007
México, UNAM *	*Últimas canciones* [Last Songs]	20′ 52′′	Richard Strauss	2007
México, UNAM *	*Fugacidad* [Fleetingness]	7′ 45′′	Frederick Chopin	2008
México, UNAM *	*Fruta extraña* [Strange Fruit]	3′ 14′′	Holiday/Allen	2008
México, UNAM *	*Diablo con vestido azul* [Devil with the Blue Dress On]	3′ 06′′	Stevenson-Long/ MitchRyder	2008
México, UNAM *	*No me detengas* [Don't Stop me Now]	3′ 32′′	Queen	2008
México, UNAM *	*No seas cruel* [Don't Be Cruel]	2′ 06′′	Elvis Presley	2008
México, UNAM *	*La casa en llamas* [House in Flames]	5′ 02′′	Jason Webley	2008
México, UNAM *	*Rock de la cárcel* [Jailhouse Rock]	2′ 31′′	Elvis Presley	2008
México, UNAM *	*Sinfonía india* [Indian Symphony]	12′ 14′′	Carlos Chávez	2008
México, UNAM *	*Galileo*	13′ 28′′	Béla Bartók	2008
México, UNAM *	*El descenso* [The Descent]	12′	Gregorio Allegri	2008

* Works Choreographed by Gloria Contreras as a member of UNAM

Ballets Created for Opera, Musical Comedy, Television and the TCUNAM School

Premier	Ballet	Music	Year
Nueva York	*Pescadores de perlas* [Pearl Fishermen]	Georges Bizet	1961
Nueva York	*Carmen*	Georges Bizet	1961
Nueva York	*Saintmaker's Christmas Eve*	Dello Joio	1961
Philadelphia	*Carmen (nueva versión)*	Georges Bizet	1962
Baltimore	*Carmen (nueva versión)*	Georges Bizet	1963
Washington	*Annie, Get Your Gun*	Irving Berlin	1963
Washington	*Gypsy*	Stephen Sondheim-Jule Stune	1963
México	*Juana de Arco en la hoguera*	Arthur Honegger	1984
Seminario del Taller Coreográfico	*Brandenburgo N° 2*	Juan Sebastián Bach	1990
Seminario del Taller Coreográfico	*Danza* [Dance]	Juan Sebastián Bach	1990

Note: All English-language titles set in brackets above are translations of the choreographed works; these titles may vary from those of the respective composers' original musical compositions.

Biographical Notes

Gloria Contreras, (b. 1934, Mexico City), has distinguished herself as a dancer, teacher, choreographer, and dance promoter. She began her dance career in Mexico as a student of Nelsy Dambré. After a brief period in Winnipeg, Canada (1955–1956), in mid-1957 she moved to New York, where she became a disciple of George Balanchine, and also studied with Pierre Vladimiroff, Felia Doubrovska, Anatole Oboukhoff, Muriel Stuart, and Carola Trier. She choreographed for the New York City Ballet, the Joffrey Ballet and the Royal Winnipeg Ballet as well as other professional companies in the United States and abroad. While in New York, she founded and directed the Gloria Contreras Dance Company (1958–1970). In the sixties she created ballets in Chile, Argentina and Brazil. When she returned to Mexico, in 1970, she founded the Taller Coreográfico de la UNAM (Universidad Nacional Autónoma de México), in Mexico City, which she directs to the present day.

Contreras has choreographed more than 210 works, whose sources range from twelfth-century scores to contemporary music. These pieces have been interpreted by close to 20 professional companies in Argentina, Brazil, Canada, Chile, Cuba, Mexico, Puerto Rico, Russia, and the United States. Contreras has formally reinvigorated Mexican ballet, and, through its content, has helped give it a contemporary face, producing several works, such as her signature piece *Huapango*, that today are considered classics of Mexican dance.

Gloria Contreras has received awards including the prestigious Premio Universidad Nacional, in 1995, for artistic creation and dissemination of culture, granted by the Universidad Nacional Autónoma de México (UNAM). In 1998 she was anointed *Artist Emeritus* of Mexico and in 2002 she was admitted as a member of Mexico's Art Academy.

She has been cited in *The Oxford Dictionary of Ballet*, and has been the subject of books such as *Gloria Contreras, Phenomenon of Mexican Ballet* (St. Petersburg, 2000), *A New Tradition in Dance* (Mexico City, 1996), by Manuel Blanco, and *Dancing the Marvelously Real* (Mexico City, 1997), by K. Mitchell Snow, among others.

K. Mitchell Snow (translator) is the author of *Dancing the Marvelously Real* as well as an art critic and contributing editor for *Américas* and correspondent for *Art Nexus*.

Lucinda Gutiérrez (translator) has worked as a translator, principally from English to Spanish, for various Mexican publishers, publications, and institutions. From 1992 to 1997, she served as a translator for the Taller Coreográfico de la UNAM.

Roberto Mata, (translator) the son of the late composer and conductor Eduardo Mata, lives in Mexico City.

Daniel Shapiro (editor) is a poet and translator. His translation of Tomás Harris's *Cipango* is forthcoming from Bucknell University Press. He is Director of Literature and Editor of *Review: Literature and Arts of the Americas* at the Americas Society in New York.

www.ingramcontent.com/pod-product-compliance
Lightning Source LLC
Chambersburg PA
CBHW021335090426
42742CB00008B/610